MW00884011

Dearest Chas,
Thank yo
sharing you
d love with
love,
Marg on.
9-18-202

Moving Forward

Moving Forward

WITH, THROUGH, AND PAST CANCER

Margaret Lang

XULON PRESS ELITE

Xulon Press
2301 Lucien Way #415
Maitland, FL 32751
407.339.4217
www.xulonpress.com

© 2020 by Margaret Lang

All rights reserved solely by the author. The author guarantees all contents are original and do not infringe upon the legal rights of any other person or work. No part of this book may be reproduced in any form without the permission of the author. The views expressed in this book are not necessarily those of the publisher.

Unless otherwise indicated, Scripture quotations taken from the King James Version (KJV) –*public domain.*

Scriptures taken or scripture quotations taken from *The Everyday Life Bible.* by Joyce Meyer., copyright © 2013. Reprinted by permission of **Faith Words.**, an imprint of Hachette Book Group., Inc.

Printed in the United States

Paperback ISBN-13: 978-1-6322-1026-5
Ebook ISBN-13: 978-1-6322-1027-2

TABLE OF CONTENTS

INTRODUCTION

I asked God in prayer about sharing my healing journey and the support and many opportunities I experienced. I was concerned that many do not have the resources, friends, and family with which I have been blessed. And then I heard God saying, "Keep writing. Every example of healing on your journey is evidence of My love, and it is meant for everyone, not only for you. I will show My love to all. Let Me do it. Just keep encouraging others that I am real and ready to heal them." And that is what I do every day. It is my way of saying "Thank You" to Him and everyone else who helped me heal.

> "The Lord will sustain, refresh and strengthen him on his bed of languishing; all his bed You [O Lord] will turn, change and transform in his illness."
> (Psalm 41:3 TELB)

FINDING OUT

"For there is nothing hidden that will not become evident, nor anything secret that will not be known and come out into the open." (Luke 8:17 TELB)

I panicked. Blood was gushing out of me like a highspeed faucet. I couldn't figure out where it was coming from. Then I looked into the toilet and saw only red. What was I supposed to do? I was visiting my daughter, Stephanie, in another state, in her daughter's bathroom, and had no access to paper towels—only toilet paper and Kleenex. My only thought was how to get it all cleaned up without a trace – without making a mess – without soiling her towels. I managed it.

You would think that I would have shared that disturbing incident with her or someone. I never did. I don't know what I was thinking except that maybe if I didn't talk about it, I would not create more trouble. You see, my daughter and I were trying to make a very tense relationship work. I didn't want to cause any alarm or more trouble and decided I would simply mention it to the doctor at my yearly checkup and then forget about it.

My yearly checkup came. I had a "fill-in" doctor with whom I was not connected. Because I felt I should tell about all my physical conditions, which were not many at the time, I simply reported the incident and suggested that it was probably just hemorrhoids. She didn't seem concerned, and I immediately dropped it. Oh, how I wish I had not.

Almost two years to the date after the first incident, I found more blood in the toilet. This time it was a very small amount. I wasn't alarmed, just concerned, because at that time I was undergoing immense pain in my leg. It was so bad that I needed a motorized chair in my house to get from room to room. I had been diagnosed with scoliosis and stenosis and had undergone five weeks of decompression and several injections in the spine for pain without relief. I was in such severe pain that I spent most of the day on the floor rubbing my leg with only intermittent times of being functional.

When I saw the relatively small amount of blood that August of 2018, I wanted to dismiss it as another sign that I was a complete mess (and maybe an alarmist, and maybe a hypochondriac). However, something told me to get it checked out but not to tell anyone. At that time, Sue was in the picture, not a family member, so I asked her to drive me to the appointment. The familiar and trusted family doctor checked me and confirmed that there was something suspicious in my rectum. It was my seventy-sixth birthday the next day. I called for a colonoscopy. By divine favor, there was a cancellation, so I could have an appointment the next week. When the doctor's assistant heard my concern, she said that it was probably not cancer, just a polyp. And why did she think that? Because she said that polyps take about two years to become cancerous. It was exactly two years prior that the blood had gushed, which I had ignored. The obvious was too clear to ignore again.

I should have taken the gushing blood sign seriously. I should have insisted on a colonoscopy instead of dismissing it. I had lessons to learn. I was JUST beginning to learn.

The colonoscopy proved that there was a growth. I had to see a gastrointestinal doctor, who, after a quick and somewhat embarrassing exam, said I had cancer. My reaction was all reason—no emotion. I asked questions about the treatment. I was sure they could just go in and cut it out. But no. He said the cure rate was far better with chemotherapy and radiation. It would take about five weeks. Then I had to wait about two months for another colonoscopy and biopsy.

I suppose some people think "death" when they hear the word "cancer." I never did. I just worried about how I was going to get through the treatment with all the intense, constant pain in my leg. How was I to endure more pain and more interruption of my life? How was I going to get through it? I never got those questions answered clearly because they were questions about the unknowable. I realized and still realize that I can do nothing without the help of grace and God. And that helping doesn't always come in the moment. It comes as an abiding commitment, moment by moment, to know—really know—that it is not by my strength, but by His.

Not long ago another dear and way-too-young friend called to tell me she had breast cancer. The reason I bring it up is because she was calling to thank me for encouraging her not to wait until she saw any physical signs that did not bode well. So, contrary to her usual behavior, she made an appointment with a doctor who found the cancer early enough to treat it.

I encourage you to listen to the signs the Holy Spirit is giving you. He is dwelling inside you and talking to you, leading you and guiding you. The Scripture warns us to be aware and listen. "For to be carnally minded *is* death; but to be spiritually minded is life and peace." (Rom. 8:6 KJV)

I told my daughter yesterday that I was going to write about my miraculous healing. She said it was urgent, "Because, Mom, so many people are dying." I shuddered. Yes, there are way too many who need to know there are exceptions, and I am one of them–to give hope and conviction that healing is our right under the covenant promises if we accept Him as our Lord and Savior.

I call myself a "walking miracle." It is true. I am healed of cancer, of back pain, and of a skin condition. All of that is true. But one of the most important healings has to do with my children.

Before the cancer diagnosis, which came in late August of 2018, I was searching for an answer to a depression and a feeling that there was nothing to look forward to. I don't think most of us take the time to find out, and certainly don't want to admit, that we are depressed. It can be a kind of blankness—a feeling that "I've already done that so I'm not really interested," or "I already have one of those and don't need another." However, with the intense and incapacitating pain from my L-4 and L-5 pinching my nerve, the darkness was inescapable. My friend, Pam, the one who saw me through my life's joys and disappointments, tried all kinds of means to figure out just what was at the bottom of my ennui. One day, she brought over an assignment that Tony Robbins had introduced in his teaching. She asked me to list all the facts about my daughter. The list became a nightmare list of huge catastrophes in our relationship. Pam said that the items on my list were *not* facts; rather, they were a list of hurts and judgements. However, she asked me to read it really fast—first from the top, and then starting at the bottom. I read it out loud really fast. Then she asked me to find circus music on my phone and play it while reading those (what I thought to be awful things) really fast. I did and started *laughing,* really laughing out loud. I could hardly finish the list without a belly laugh. What seemed so horrible in the past was really just nothing and really funny. There was no more attachment to the pain of it in the present. Something had happened. I was over the whole drama and regret. What happened in the past, just happened. It had no more painful hold on me. I was released, and what a good feeling that was!

The Bible says that the joy of the Lord is our strength (Neh. 8:10). One thing I need to say about that is His is the timing and the answer. I have learned to depend on knowing that.

Actually, that was not the end of it all. It was just the beginning of a hope that things would be different in the future. And the real message turned out to be that the hurt, disappointment, and sense of failure in my life were not due to the relationships with my girls, but the guilt I had inflicted on myself because of their dad divorcing me years and years ago. (That story will unfold.) However, it gave me great relief to get to the bottom of the sadness and disappointment that I had covered up all my life. And I know I will repeat this, but at the bottom of my depression was the failure I felt about that failed marriage. Believe it or not, the cancer—the horrible, malignant intrusion in my rectum—was the very life-stealing tumor I was going to heal, just like the life-stealing belief of failure had been in my life. I was finally at the bottom of it.

WHERE DOES IT COME FROM?

Many months after my healings, I was at a party with past clients who had not seen me without my long, white hair, which had been my claim to beauty fame. They told me how much younger I looked, and I shared that I felt so much younger as well. Two of them in particular, each separately, took my hand and said that it was my strong spirit that had made me well. They were acknowledging the strength in my spirit, my determination, my willingness to surrender to the Great Physician. I wondered about where that spirit came from and was reminded of my mom and dad.

They left me a great legacy of love. The most prominent memory of that was the night years ago when I went to Rockford from Chicago with my two babies. I was in a complete depression from the divorce, reeling from the fact that their dad did not love me anymore. I had lost ten pounds in a week and desperately needed Mom and Dad's warm embrace to assure me that I could survive. We sat at the dinner table as we had so often while I was growing up. Something possessed me to ask them if I could move in and live with them. I never doubted that they would say "yes." My mom shocked me when she said, "You go give the babies a bath, and Dad and I will talk about it." My mom never said "no" to me about a need I had. They were supporting us financially through the divorce proceedings and paid for the last courses I needed to take at Loyola to become a teacher. I was stunned by her response. I took the babies to the bathtub, sat on the floor and waited. Soon they came to the bathroom door and stood there, Dad's arm around Mom, and said that

I could stay. There were no conditions. Just stay. Looking at them, as I do in my mind to this day, realizing the love and generosity they shared, gave me the greatest hope I have ever known. I had felt so betrayed by my husband; I had lost trust. Yet here were two people reaching out, extending their love, and my faith in human kindness was restored. I looked at them through tears and said, "Because of your strength, even in the midst of Dad's battle with prostate cancer, and because of your love, I can leave. You have renewed my strength."

I found that story important because I was sure it was one of the turning points in my life that solidified my spirit and hope. It certainly reminds me of how much we can affect others' lives. I am sure that the spiritual strength that got me through cancer was related to that memory. I am certain that having experiences of belief in something greater than our pain is what makes us strong. But in reconsidering, for some of us, past memories may not be very immediate nor helpful in the times of great stress, fear, or pain.

So, I have had to ask myself: Without being able to rely on good memories, where do we get a strong spirit? Where did my faith come from during the process? The obvious answer is prayer, the Word of God and His promises, and faith. What I also have come to believe is that I had to commit to a principle of never being a victim.

One major revelation happened years ago when I was reading *The Course of Miracles*. One of the lessons was: "Would you rather be right or happy?" Wow. I read that when I was in the aftermath of the horrible divorce, feeling more like a victim than ever before. I was a single mom with two adopted kids, always nervous and wondering about whether the check for child support would come. I was teaching at a school with lots of female colleagues who offered me sympathy. I was the perfect, classic case of a lost, woebegone victim, and they were more than happy to console me and remind me that my situation was horrible. It was so tempting to succumb to their concern. They meant so well, but they were reinforcing my belief in suffering, of being a victim. I had to change my mind. I had to choose happiness instead of being right about my situation.

And I made the choice. I remember the exact place where I made that decision. There was no alternative for me because something deep inside knew that changing my belief was my only hope. I had to *see* everything differently. I had to consciously change each thought of "woe is me" to "everything happens for more." It is that thought that gave me the most hope because it put me in charge of how I saw the situation. It gave me control. I had been out of control. I was a victim of him, the courts, the whole horrible betrayal. I did not see myself as the center of my life. I was the half of a marriage without the other half. I was weak, dependent, and terrified.

I had to change all my thinking. I had to watch my thoughts. I find, as I am writing, that no matter what the subject, the Bible has already addressed it. In this case, it does so in Second Corinthians which reads, "Casting down imaginations, and every high thing that exalteth itself against the knowledge of God, and bringing into captivity every thought to the obedience of Christ." (II Corinthians 10:5 KJV) To be obedient to Christ, I had to see myself as He sees me: perfect in His sight because of His redeeming blood on the cross.

I am fortified with knowing Scripture. For those of you who are not there yet, I am sure you will find that the Bible teachings are really common sense. And for now, hold on to that. Being in control of our thoughts puts us in control of our lives. It gives strength. We can begin to ask questions about why something is happening in our lives and how we can use those happenings to make something better. The Bible even talks about that. In Romans 8:28, it says, "We are assured and know that [God being a partner in their labor] all things work together and are [fitting into a plan] for good to and for those who love God and are called according to [His] design and purpose." (TELB) In other words, all of us have the ability to see that everything is an opportunity for greater good. This is a hard fact when we find ourselves in great pain or grief. I just have to again reaffirm my *choice* to believe that either immediately or eventually, I will see or receive something good from bad. It is a decision that I made and continue to make, and in my case, I depend on the Holy Spirit to give me that insight and revelation. And to believe it will happen in His time. In the meantime, I just keep on reminding myself of all of the above.

Preparing for the Big Race

After the appointment with the gastrointestinal doctor, the next step was the oncologist's office. And there I did sense death. There were so many patients, more than I could ever imagine. There were numbers of them sitting in chairs getting chemo. Looking at the poles and cords and tubes and shaved heads, a spirit of heaviness came over me. I don't think I felt the heaviness for myself just yet. I was still in a state of semi-denial and felt as though I were in charge of everything having to do with my treatment. I hadn't surrendered yet to the Divine Physician through the hands, brains, and hearts of so many caregivers.

So, with an attitude like "I can handle this," and "I will direct it," I told the doctor that I could not go through the treatment schedule without first taking care of the pain in my leg. To give myself credit, it seemed impossible. I had endured so much pain. I had given up so much of everyday life because of it. It was so bad that one time when I was sitting in the passenger seat of my friend's car at a stoplight, I said, "Just wait a moment." I jumped out of the car and got in the backseat just to lie down and rub my leg. My need for relief was that urgent.

My oncologist did not like my attitude. I was a bit impudent, like I knew better that he did. So, he took his computer and slammed it shut, saying, "Well, go get your leg fixed and then come back, and we will deal with the cancer."

My dearest friend, Pam, was in the exam room with us and exclaimed, "No. We will not wait. Cancer treatment first!" The doctor told me months later that very few people have a friend like her. She listened to what I could not hear at the time. She could hear with ears that were not stopped up with fear, even fear in denial.

He outlined his method of treatment. The words were clear, but it felt like they came through the static in my head that said, "This can't be happening to me." Yet there it was, the outline of a plan for five weeks of treatment. First, I had to have a surgical procedure for the insertion of a port in my chest. Then the radiation would start, five days a week, for five weeks. During that time, I would get two weeks of chemotherapy. Next, I was sent to radiology.

What did I know at this stage of the journey? I asked the radiologist about it. He said that my cancer treatment was like a marathon —very grueling, very tiring, very trying. And that some people just quit. That idea never occurred to me. The day-to-day posed a lot of challenges, like a marathon does, but in both you know how far the race is ahead of time and have pretty much decided to do it. There are also markers on the way. One mile, mile two, and so on. I had something like that in the form of a calendar on the wall to mark off the days, five weeks of days. Each night I would put a big black "X" on the date, showing my progress.

A long time ago, my best friend's dad died. I was at their home before going to the service. His mom was in heavy grieving. My friend had the wisdom to say, "Once this day is over, we will never have to go through it again." I used that idea a lot during my chemo and radiation.

Step 1: The Port and a Tuna Fish Sandwich

Each time there was a scheduled procedure, the sky was still dark, and it was cold outside when it was time to go. I often wondered why. I had to dispel the darkness affecting my attitude as we proceeded to the hospital to have an incision in my chest and a port inserted for the chemo.

Sue, my friend and neighbor, was right on time to pick me up. My little dog kept barking for Sue to walk her, but we didn't have time. You see, Molly has always loved Sue. It all started one day when I was trying to walk her while I was on a scooter, getting off only to pick up what Molly had left behind. I still thought I could do things by myself, even though some tasks were intensely difficult. That's when a car came around the corner, slowed down, stopped, and Sue asked, "Margaret, is there anything I can do for you?"

At that time, I was still in the mindset of being able to handle everything by myself. As a single mom, I had years of practice. So, my response was, "No, thanks; I'm fine." Then I reconsidered. "Wait. There is something I would like. Could you please vacuum my house for me?" I usually ran the vacuum each day, at least in all the traffic areas.

Sue responded immediately. "Sure. Do you want me to come today?" I was so relieved and happy. Sure enough, that day started with me accepting some help and grew to being able to receive MUCH help. All the time I had been in denial of what I could do on my own. God has such a sweet way of teaching us to accept His help through others.

I believe they are His appointed angels. Sue became my angel and one of my best friends.

But we weren't there yet. You see, she was helping me because of my back pain. We didn't know about the cancer yet. That came later, after two months of her coming over each day to walk the dog, water the flowers, feed the birds, fix whatever needed fixing, and pick up groceries. Her "service" then evolved into becoming a caretaker of perfection beyond measure.

So, there we were on the way to the hospital for the first procedure to prepare for the insertion of chemo. Because Sue had taken care of her mother for so many years before she passed away, it seemed like she knew the ins and outs of every medical piece of information I was given. Her mom had a series of major issues. Sue is also a researcher, and she looks up everything that is presented to her. However—and this is a big "however"—she never scared me with what she knew. She only reassured me, and only if I asked.

I am not a big "needing to know" person when it comes to anything medical. I came from a medical family. My dad being a radiologist and my mom a nurse, we had plenty of reminders of cancer and other ailments around us all the time. I had decided a long time ago to block out all of that discussion and focus. I was going to be well by thinking positively and asking God for healing. However, having Sue with me to know about medical things was comforting. Even if I didn't ask, I knew she would tell me if I needed to know something critical.

Back to the early morning journey to get the port. Hospitals are not hospitality centers for sure! Bright lights, steel carts and chairs, and no color is what I remember. I had to be in a wheelchair and remember going down a very long hall. I was thinking at the time that I could never have walked it. Then the waiting began —maybe an hour at least before checking in, all the time in a room filled with people. Again, as had happened so many times, I was overwhelmed by the sight of so many people enduring so much pain. I will never get over those images, and I pray for all of them whenever the image comes back.

Finally, they called me to register (even though we had registered downstairs upon entering). Then another wait, filled with mounting tension until they finally called me into the pre-op room. They put me in a gown, tucked away my phone, offered me a warm blanket, and left me to wait again. I noticed that my blood pressure was very high. Then, of course, I had to use the restroom. I remember that they were remodeling, so I had to walk quite a distance to use the bathroom. That was the first trip of four! Why? Because the doctor was in another procedure and couldn't be reached for permission to give me the medicine to relax before the surgery. I was very anxious. And cold. The blanket had long lost its warmth. There was no phone for a quick meditation tape. I very well know the Scripture "Be still and know that I am God" (Ps. 46:10 KJV), but to tell the truth, anticipating what is coming and yet not knowing exactly what it is makes it very difficult to "be still." Proverbs 12:25 says, "Anxiety in a man's heart weighs it down, but an encouraging word makes it glad." (TELB) An "encouraging word" at that moment would have been, "Just go home. You don't need this. You don't have cancer." In all honesty, I actually considered just getting up and leaving. I would really like to know how many of you have had that same thought.

I have always given myself permission to just leave something or somewhere if I chose, but this was different. I knew that I had to stay and see this whole treatment through. I do know some who say that they would never go through chemo and radiation. However, that would not be me. I never seriously considered giving up at any time during the process and was reminded of that yesterday by my good friend, Pam. We were at the oncologist's office, where she watched a man being lifted by three people back into his car. "He has given up," she observed. She is the kind of person who knows things like that. And then she added, "You were never like that. You never gave up." And that is why we were leaving the oncology clinic having received the good news that I was cancer free, and I have been for more than a year.

Back to the gurney and waiting for the port. After what seemed like an eternity (which was actually about three hours), they gave me the sedative, and soon I was waking up with a metal cylinder thing in my chest. It hurt, but not that bad. And then I looked up, and there was Sue, smiling and asking if I were hungry and if I wanted a tuna fish sandwich. No food ever has sounded so good. I ate every bite in the car on the way home, famished and relieved that it was over, even though I knew it was just the beginning. I was relieved and renewed because of a friend who thought to bring me a tuna fish sandwich. That kind of support would bring me through.

We know that He said He would never leave nor forsake us. (Joshua 1:5) He actually commanded us to be strong. "Have I not commanded you? Be strong, vigorous, and very courageous. Be not afraid, neither be dismayed, for the Lord your God is with you wherever you go." (Joshua 1:9 TELB)

He kept His promise to me. As He was with the Israelites in the desert by day with a cloud and fire by night, He was always near me with His loving and tender presence.

Warrior Woman

M any months after the chemo and radiation, an elder in my church called me "Warrior Woman" as I stood in front of her. Those words have resonated in me since. She said she saw me with a huge shield which I was holding with little effort. It served as my protection as I was on the offense, battling whatever the devil put in front of me. That was her vision.

And then I remembered. What I saw was me lying on the cold table in the radiation room with the huge metal apparatus stationed overhead. My stomach had been tattooed for the exact mark for the radiation. Many serious and disciplined minds had figured out what that machine could do and what it was supposed to do for me. I had no idea of what they had figured out. I was just a body under a huge, medical machine, all by myself while the nurses were in safe enclosures. I felt so small. I was cold no matter how solicitous the nurses had been to make me comfortable. Ten minutes each time, five times a week for five weeks.

And it began. It swirled around on the ceiling. I watched it go from one side to the other and back again. A metal giant overhead injecting something into my body to make the growth inside it go away. I was overwhelmed. Scared. Alone. And it made an eerie sound. It was not anything human to relate to. I couldn't talk to it. I was under it. I was totally out of control.

And then the words and thoughts came which I used so often. "Not my strength, Lord, but Yours." I found those words on page 30 of Keith Moore's book on healing, *God's Will To Heal*. I copied them like this:

He gives me unyielding strength,
Impenetrable strength.
He gives me unfailing strength.
He makes me strong.
He gives me strength.
I will go in the strength of the Lord God.
He gives me strength.

I had posted them above the sink in the kitchen, and they are still there today. However, with that machine hovering over me, all I could think and say to myself was, "It is You, Lord, not me. You enable me to be strong. You enable me to withstand all this stress. You are so strong inside me that my cells are absorbing only the radiation I need for healing. You, Lord, not me."

I recognize today that the thought of His strength inside me was my shield. My body was not being invaded to the point of being hurt because His strength was already there, keeping the balance. The radiation was put in me. He was already in my body, ready to heal me. Without knowing of God's presence in each of my cells, I believe the fear would have overwhelmed me, and the healing process would certainly have been impeded. I was being healed from the inside out.

But it wasn't over yet. The radiation treatment itself did not cause me any pain. There was emotional pain in seeing all the contraptions, like skulls they used to put on patients with brain tumors. They weren't funny. However, looking at them made me feel grateful that they were not for me.

The negative results from radiation came at the end of the five weeks in the form of severe burns on my buttocks. The color was a reddish brown, and the skin was literally peeling. I could not sit. The only position somewhat comfortable was lying down. I had open sores in the groin area besides and wondered how they ever could be healed. How, especially in that area, was skin going to grow to recover those open wounds? This was my worst time.

I really had doubts about those sores healing. Salve on. Sitz baths. Fan pointing to the infected region. My routine was one of waiting. However, I never stopped exercising on the floor. Then I stayed there listening to motivation tapes. They were from Brain Tap and a Dr. Patrick

Porter. They suggested looking forward to a time when I was healed. The most important part of listening was the passing of time. There was nothing I could do myself to heal. I had to wait for the process to take effect. And, of course, I listened to Joel Olsteen, Joseph Prince, and Kenneth Copeland. All this would take me to about 11:00 AM. Then came the Sitz bath, and then the whole day ahead with nothing I could do, including sitting while reading the Bible. This was the most difficult time. A prisoner of healing! What a concept. Time dragging along. Another day to practice mind control and to visualize what it would be like to have it over.

Time was my savior and my demon. For someone who had planned each hour as a teacher with bells ringing to change classes every fifty minutes, I was a creature of goal-setting and accomplishment. But not then. Time was necessary to heal me. Time was torturing me with the waiting.

And that is when I realized that my mind was in a totally new and different place. Yes, I had my audio tapes and lots of Scripture reeling in my head, but I was really somewhere else. I was in what Billye Brim called a "bubble." One time I heard her describe the shock and grief of her husband dying very young. She said that God placed her in a "bubble." Somehow, she got through the shock and grief in a peaceful and protected way until she was ready to face the reality of her new life. I believe God placed me in a bubble during the healing time from the cancer treatment. The Holy Spirit changed my clock. He put me in a holy mindset that allowed me to endure the painful healing time. It took a "bubble" to believe that my body would heal, as difficult as it was to believe it when I looked at my open sores.

There were times, though, when just knowing that my friend, Pam, would be over to my house at around four in the afternoon soothed me. Something to mark the time when time had no definition. One night I was lying in bed looking at the ceiling which is textured into patterns. I looked up and saw His face made out of that random design. And that was the time when I said, "Ok, God. This is it. I cannot go on much longer like this. You must do something. I can't. I am making a deep and irrevocable decision to be well. Yes, I am well, and I am going to get better quickly from this time on." I did not hear an answer, of course, from the ceiling. I heard it in my heart and knew I was already on the way. And I was. He always answers.

My radiologist had told me right at the beginning that going through radiation was like running a marathon. You had to decide to do it and never quit until the end. Whenever I hear the word "marathon," I think of the book *Marathon Man* by William Goldman. In the novel, there is a torture scene where a character has his teeth drilled out without any anesthetic. I really didn't expect the radiation to be that bad, but the endurance it called for was certainly nothing less than what is expected when running a marathon. The funny part, and there always is for me, is that I was planning a trip to Disney before the diagnosis, at exactly the time for the last radiation treatment. My friend asked if I would be able to go on the trip as planned. The doctor just looked at us and said, "Well, she can go, but I don't think she will want to." He was absolutely right!

Radiation and its aftermath were bad, but never as bad as having all my teeth drilled out! You could say that my belief was that things could be worse. I know some people think that way to make themselves feel better, but I never do. I always believe that something better is going to come out of any bad situation. It always does for me because that is what I focus on going through anything.

Radiation brought me physical healing from cancer, as well as a healing of the very sad and bad relationship with my daughter, Stephanie. She had come from Indiana at this worst time to help me. She came with horrible baggage from the past—pain and a sense of isolation. But she came. We both decided to let it go, all of it. I told her that I didn't blame her for any anger she held and only felt sorry that the past could not be redone. My decision was to go forward with every breathing moment I had left without the past and in total and deliberate joy. That was the commitment I had made. I asked her if she wanted to go on that new journey together. She said, "Yes," and our friendship, love, and appreciation for each other deepens with joy each and every day.

Who says that cancer kills everything? Cancer gave me the chance to have a daughter again.

I want to say more about Stephanie. I see her as very unusual. Years ago, when her only daughter, Kate, was a baby of six months, Stephanie sensed there was something terribly wrong with her. After a spasm and a harrowing ride in the ambulance, which took a wrong turn, they finally got to the hospital. There the baby was diagnosed with AVM, or arteriovenous malformation. To fix it required brain surgery. Three surgeries, in fact. I witnessed my daughter's faith and grace throughout the whole ordeal and her daughter's—my granddaughter's—complete healing. Even after this life and death experience, our relationship was seriously strained.

Yet, when I told her about my cancer diagnosis, she immediately asked if she could fly to Arizona and help me. The visit was scheduled for a few weeks later. Then it arrived in the mail: the very prayer book I had given her when my granddaughter was undergoing surgery, so many years before. It was exactly like mine, the one I was using each day to pray for my healing. In the card that came with it, she'd written, "Mom, I have carried this everywhere since you gave it to me years ago, and now I hope it will help you." For all those many years of grief, tension, and sadness about our relationship, we were both carrying the same little book and praying the same prayers.

God never left us. He was always in the middle, connecting us, just waiting for the right time.

He Tied My Shoe

Many months later, we were standing in the laundry room by the backdoor. Sue was on her way out, putting on her shoes. A smile came across her face that looked like pure joy.

"What?" I asked.

"Well," she said, "I was walking my dog and came across a home being remodeled. I asked if I could see it, but I had the dog, who is terrified of walking on tile floors. There was only tile in the house. I picked up the dog and was holding her when the young man who let me in said, 'Your shoe is untied. Let me tie your shoe.' And he did." My heart just leapt at the wonderful vision of my friend having someone, a complete stranger, stoop down, completely unasked, to tie her shoe.

Such a sweet, unexpected, right-to-the-heart act of kindness. That story made me think and feel of so many such acts that I received during my healing journey. One is on my mind often. I call it "the hand in the night." I was in a great deal of pain after the operation, so they had me on a regimen of heavy-duty pills every four hours. I always heard the doctors and nurses say, "Don't let the pain get ahead of you." They said the same of nausea. Those cautions made me quite disciplined about taking my meds. Better than an abrupt, sharp alarm clock was the sweet, soft touch and sweet, soft voice in the middle of the night reminding me it was time for another pill. The soft touch came, and then, "Mom, it is time to take your pill." Catherine's touch and her voice reassured me that I was taken care of and loved. That act went right to my heart.

Then I thought of Karen standing in the very hot sun on a 110-degree day with the prayer cloth she had asked the pastors to pray over. I couldn't get out of the car because of the pain in my leg. I couldn't walk into the church where she worked to get it. So, there she stood, waiting for me to roll down the window for the prized prayer cloth. That little cloth held such tender reminders of her kindness, gentle and loving. She had reached out to the pastors to pray over it for me and saw to it I received it from her loving hands.

Sometime into my chemo, while resting at home, a knock came at the door. Mary stood there, a neighbor I didn't know well at the time. She offered me a bouquet of flowers and a brief greeting with love for healing. The beautiful flowers were just the beginning of the beautiful friendship we have developed. We now have a relationship of friendship that, before the cancer, may have never happened.

Then there was the call from Mary Ellen. She and I had an argument years before. I knew she had health problems herself. What she called for was to find out what kind of soup I liked. Soup to be homemade, delivered to the door, with only concern and well wishes. And she was in pain herself. I could relate to how it must have felt to make that soup while hurting. It didn't seem to matter to her, though, because that is what she wanted to do. It was delicious. We have since become much better friends. That act of kindness spoke way more than any harsh words ever had. New doors to the heart were being built by an offer and acceptance of a pot of soup.

"Are you really serious about covering my plants?" I asked Sue, while in the hospital bed after the operation. I had never asked her to do that, and to tell the truth, I wouldn't have known that the temperature was going down under 36 degrees that night. Something about not having to think about those plants and knowing someone would take care of them touched me to the core. Reaching out is what she did. Seeing something to be done and doing it just because it needed doing. Another example of tying a shoe or reaching out during the night.

Thinking about the command to "love our neighbor as ourselves" reminds me of Georgiann, our Book Club leader. I was so touched when each month she called, right on schedule, to ask if I were well enough to attend the meeting. She never forgot me. I will always remember.

And then there was Annie. After a long day at the vet clinic clear across town, she came by to pick up Molly, took her home and groomed her. My little baby dog was returned looking elegant, fluffy and loved. Annie's sweetness and her transforming my dog filled my heart each time. Her loving spirit filled me with strength and hope. If Molly could look so much better after being groomed, I thought there was hope for me!

There were so many instances of surprise visits while I was sick, like the Sunday morning when I was on the couch, and my two neighbors asked if they could stop by. One is ninety-seven years old; the other is ninety-five. "Of course," I told them. "Please come." It took a while for them to arrive, because one of them can only walk with a walker, and even with it quite laboriously. Besides the heroic trek to my door, they were dressed in their Sunday best. Neither wore a hat. I noticed that because they reminded me of years past when we all dressed with hats and white gloves for church. With neither hats nor gloves, and very modern, these two had an aura of years of prayer and even holiness. I thought they looked beautiful. One had on a blouse buttoned up to the neck with a beautiful broach. The other wore a lovely suit. Both couldn't wait to share their devotion for the day which came up naturally in conversation because they were excited about the new book they were studying by Rick Warren. I am still amazed at their courage, their love, their interest in life, their looking for more from life by studying. These two angels appeared on my doorstep to give me an example of graceful aging and sparks of joy. I will never forget that Sunday sermon acted out by two wonderful women of God.

I am reminded, too, of Thanksgiving, when I had so much anxiety about being able to sit at their table. Days before, I had stressed about how I was to be a good guest. I was going to Darla's and knew I could ask to lie down if needed but felt embarrassed to ask. The day came. I went. I will always remember her sweetness and her husband Nick's concern as they pillowed the sofa with comfort for me. I would sit at the table and then go lie down. Her sweet face would stand over me pouring love into me and reassuring me that I was not a "problem." That Thanksgiving will always have a special meaning for me.

About that time Christmas was nearing. Who rang the bell? It was my neighbor, Susan, knocking at the door. She is a crafter, whom, even after living across the street for eleven years, I hardly knew. She brought me a gift that she had made: a darling Christmas elf to hang on my door. Such a generous gift which, since being delivered, has brought us closer and closer. From "across-the-street neighbors" who just said "hi," we have become dear friends.

During all this time, my pastor and his wife stood by my side. They anointed me with oil and claimed I would be healed from the top of my head to the soles of my feet. Their confidence in the fact that God hears and answers prayer sustained me constantly.

What does all this add up to? He said He would never leave nor forsake us. Here He is—right in our midst, manifesting Himself to us through a neighbor, a friend, a pastor, a stranger. He is always reaching out for us to receive His blessing.

The other day, my nephew, Dane, was telling me how he prays each night. I asked if he could write it down. He did. I was overwhelmed with the ending most of all and have made it my daily prayer.

"Jesus, please give us an awareness of and a commitment to live like You. Give us the strength, patience, understanding, and love to operate as You do in every aspect of our lives and in every relationship! No offense taken, just wisdom, patience, and love."

Cancer, pain and suffering offer so many opportunities to love. To give it and receive it, just like Jesus!

MESSAGES IN THE BLOOD

S eeing blood where it should not have been was the first indica-
tion that something was terribly wrong in my body. It was a signal,
a warning sign that saved my life. Because of it I made those doctor
appointments and was on my way to curing the cancer.

I saw lots more blood but then in protected vials taken out of my
arm. I am not sure how many times I had to go to the lab. Each time
they wrapped my upper arm and stuck in the needle, the amount of
blood which squirted into the tube amazed me. The contents of those
vials would show how I was handling the chemo. Other tests would
show if there were anything lacking that would prevent me from the
surgery. Others would show any allergies. The message of healing, health
or sickness was measured by the blood. Again, as before, the blood was
the messenger.

My respect for the amount of my blood grew and grew. I never worried that there would not be enough. It just kept coming, each time, as
much as they needed. I was in awe that my body would make up for what
they took, make up for the missing blood, that it would restore itself.

There is no doubt that all that confrontation with blood made me
think of His blood shed for me on the cross. I believe that with His
blood, He took all my sins on Himself and redeemed me completely
from past, present, and future sins, just because I have accepted Him
as my Lord and Savior. Whenever I think of all He suffered for me and
that He loved me so much, my faith in His healing power in my body is
strengthened. He just asked me to believe.

A friend during this time told me that he believed only the Jewish people were meant to be healed. He said the Gentiles were not given that promise. I was stunned. He was questioning my belief that Jesus wanted healing for me, a Gentile. I asked myself why I was so sure that Jesus wanted me healed. (And I am sure.) The answer, for me, is because of the cross and because healing is all about what Jesus did during His ministry. Why would He have devoted so much time and compassion to heal so many if He didn't want us healed? I just cannot conceive it. His blood was completely given in the perfect sacrifice for me to be well. Does it take a lot of faith to keep believing that? No; for me it is not a matter of how much faith, but rather a decision to believe His love and His divine care for me.

To keep me grounded in my belief in His healing promises, I looked up the 101 Scriptures about God's wishes for healing for me in Keith Moore's book, *God's Will To Heal*. I printed out those Scriptures and read them aloud over and over again, reinforcing my faith with His Words. They reassured me and took my mind off the pain and worry.

Joseph Prince also taught me that Jesus took the scourging for my healing. His back became one of open bones and blood. Joseph Prince shares his belief that Jesus did not have to go through that horrible beating because the crucifixion would have been enough to satisfy the Father. He teaches that the extra stripes He took were all for our bodies to be made well.

> But He was wounded for our transgressions, He was bruised for our guilt and iniquities; the chastisement [needful to obtain] peace and well-being for us was upon Him, and with the stripes [that wounded] Him we are healed and made whole. (Isaiah 53:5 TELB)

I also meditated a lot on the woman with the issue of blood. I saw myself in her as she risked everything just to touch His garment. She didn't care what others thought of her. She knew they would even persecute her for being out among others, for she was unclean according to Jewish law. And yet she was determined to be well; she knew that she was worth it. She dared to reach out to the Source of Health. And then He asked, "Who is it who touched me?" And she "declared in the presence of all the people for what reason she had touched Him and how she had been instantly cured." (Luke 8:45, 47) She had felt, really felt, His healing power transferred from Him to her. And healing was not all she received. He further rewarded her faith in Him by saying, "Daughter, your faith (your confidence and trust in Me) has made you well! Go (enter) into peace (untroubled, undisturbed well-being)." (Luke 8:48 TELB) She was not only made well; she had her whole life restored. And that is what Jesus has done for me. I am completely well. I feel His presence. My family ties are restored. My seeping blood has been dried up in the belief in His blood. As much as I see the similarities between the woman in the Bible and myself, I envy that she got to look directly into His eyes. I close my eyes and see Him looking at me, putting myself in her place. It gives me a sweet sense of communicating with Him. It also makes me happy that I have the promise of someday doing it in person with my sweet Jesus.

Yes, blood is necessary for life. His Blood gave me back mine.

MESSY

Sickness can be really messy. I am thinking about spilled blood, the effects of incontinence, vomiting, excess mucus, dry skin left in the tub after peeling off from radiation, and on it goes. It's messy when your hair is falling out, and a friend or stranger finds it on the back of your fresh, black sweatshirt. I could get very graphic here—like describing the time I did not hang up soon enough and did not make it to the bathroom. Rectal cancer posed its own messes. Then there is the frustration, and, mostly, the embarrassment. I don't care who says, "Oh, it's ok. I am not bothered by it at all." Their saying that doesn't clean up the mess.

And then there is the mess of losing parts of the body, as my friend is anticipating next month. She has had her chemo and now faces a double mastectomy, radiation, and then a hysterectomy. She told me this with a bald head, already having lost all of her beautiful, long, long hair. Her Rapunzel princess image exists no longer. Her buxom image will disappear, at least until the replacements are installed. And her hope of having another child is completely robbed. I use that word on purpose because her whole identity before cancer was one of wife and mother. What should I say to her? What condolences can I offer?

None. There is nothing anyone can do about these messes, some more severe than others. Some occur while the person going through the disease and treatments has help; others do not. It strikes me as ironic that the procedures that precipitate all these messes are done in completely sterile environments. So interesting. Parts of our bodies are being shed. The question is: "What is left?"

That IS the question. I can only answer by using what my friend, Pam Emmer, as a teacher and researcher on the brain, came up with years ago. This may turn a lot of people off. They think the following questions are ridiculous. However, if truly pondered, they can reveal a whole new dimension of reality and goodness.

First, I have to ask: "Why did I want this?" If you are still reading, steady yourself and think about it. I believe that I must always take responsibility for my thoughts and what they create. We are far past the time when people did not believe that the thoughts produced in the brain affect the body. The Bible, in Second Corinthians 10:5, says that we must take every thought captive. That we must not worry and cast our cares on Him. Yes, thoughts create, and that is the principle to stand on steadfastly and with clarity.

Back to the question: "Why did I want this?" At the time I was going through the treatment while in great pain, which stemmed from the discs pressing on the nerve in my leg, I don't think I could have answered or even addressed the question in that condition. What I did know was that no matter why or what, I was going to determine to believe that something good was to come from it. And it did. I stood steadfastly on the promise in Romans 8:28: "And we know that all things work together for good to them that love God, to them who are the called according to His purpose." (KJV)

Only now can I see that I wanted this "process" to heal all the old wounds of the past. I cannot think about the bad in the past anymore, nor will I even allow it to be an influence or excuse in my life. The result of that decision took place on that one day when my daughter Stephanie arrived to take care of me. I have already written about our healing. However, it was so huge that I want to amplify. She was beside herself, unknown to me at the time, haunted by memories of our turbulent past and unable get her head around the fact that I had a "terminal" disease. She wanted to escape all of it, both the past it brought up and the present unpalatable situation.

She said, "Mom, I have to leave you. I can't take it."

I instantly—and I mean only for an instant—panicked. Really panicked. And then the great peace of the Holy Spirit and wisdom spoke for me, and I have never been the same. Out of my mouth came the words, "If you have to leave, I understand. I cannot change the past. I cannot redo the past. I cannot ever heal the deep wounds and the regret I hold. I just have to let it go and focus on the future, one I will create with love and joy, always looking forward. If you want to go on that new journey with me, I would relish it." That's it. That's all I said.

She got up and walked into the kitchen. I asked another question. She said, "I do not want to talk about it." And all the past was over. We have been building a closer and closer relationship with each passing day. We trust each other.

Yes, everything does happen for more. It fits the divine Word of Christ, which says, in John 10:10, "I came that they may have life and enjoy life, and have it in abundance (to the full, till it overflows)." (TELB) Today we spent two hours visiting on the phone and sharing insights. As I'm thinking about it, we did talk about the past, but it was about good things. God's Grace is amazing.

That takes me back to my friend who is still facing so much. In the world's view, she will be stripped of her femininity. What the world knows as "feminine" will be taken away: her hair, her breasts, her uterus. Thus, the question again is: "Why did she want this?" I don't think she could answer this right away; however, just asking this question will give her back a sense of control. She was in control of creating it, and she is in control of the outcome based on His Word and her perception.

Getting back to the other question: "What is left?" Her answer right now is what the Holy Spirit reveals to her. What I see is that her definition of herself as a wife and mother was way too small and limited. I see Anna Marie living in all her potential to be all that He saw in her from the creation of the world. Her husband could die; her child could grow up and leave, and she would be nothing in her mind's eye without a deeper knowing of who she is. She is being given a chance to see what is behind that too-small definition of herself. She is being given a chance to broaden her knowing of how God sees her. She can rest knowing that He sees her as perfect, and that He loves her no matter what is in the natural. And when she gets that message, (I am purposely not calling it a "lesson"), that revelation of who she is and how much she is loved and how big is her purpose, then her life will become more and more abundant just like He promised, and she will be healed.

Like it says in the Bible, from the ashes He creates a garland. He always has our good on hand and is ready to dispense it. I love His promises of restoration in Isaiah 61:3.

> [I came] To grant [consolation and joy] to those who mourn in Zion – to give them an ornament (a garland or diadem) of beauty instead of ashes, the oil of joy instead of mourning, the garment [expressive] of praise instead of a heavy, burdened, and failing spirit – that they may be called oaks of righteousness [lofty, strong, and magnificent, distinguished for uprightness, justice, and right standing with God], the planting of the Lord, that He may be glorified. (TELB)

I think I'd prefer to see myself as an "oak of righteousness" over any other role the world says I should play. As a wife and mother, sister or brother, anyone, how magnificent to be aware of the glory of the Lord shining in and through me. With this conviction, I can do all things through Christ Who strengthens me. (Philippians 4:13)

As a footnote: my joy must be radiating out of me because I am stopped often with a compliment from a complete stranger about how well I look. I always say, "I am a walking miracle because of the grace of God." And in this way, I get to share His love.

It is kind of funny to look at the physical mess and see it as ashes out of which will grow an amazing and solid tree of righteousness! I find that it is always good to see the humor in everything, including the messy poop on the floor!

WHAT ABOUT MY HAIR?

"Will it fall out with the chemo?" I asked the oncologist. He replied, "Probably, not." And then, when it started to fall out, he suggested I shave my head. That decision did not come right away.

I said to Sue one day, on the way home from an appointment, that we should stop at the wig shop just to see what they had. It was a funny experience because at that point I still had hair. For years my hair was the crowning point in my estimation of any glamor I possessed. I wore it straight back with a scrunchie, and it was marvelous, white and thick and lovely. At least that is what I always heard from people. "Oh, you have the most beautiful hair," strangers would come up to tell me. And I never had to do anything with it. No products. No fuss. Just wash, let dry, and go. So, I didn't get a wig. It was a really foreign concept at that point.

And then the threat of losing it all became a reality rather than a mere threat. That is when I made what I believe was my strongest decision. I had a very serious discussion with God. I simply told Him that my hair was the one thing in the whole ordeal I would never question or worry about. I really was able to turn it all over. Because my hair was such an important part of my feeling feminine and pretty, I knew I had to let any anxiety or worry or stress just go. I told God that He would have to take care of it and me with it. I never went back on that promise. I am very aware of the verse that says, "Casting all your care upon Him;

for He careth for you." (1 Pet. 5:7 KJV) I cannot often do it, but that time I did.

Recently, I happened to find a selfie in the gallery on my phone that showed my face during chemo. I was shocked to see my ashen face and a few strands of white hair emerging from an almost bald head. I had just a few strands tied back with the scrunchie. What was I thinking? I looked terrible. But I was hanging on to that hair. I bought hats, too, cute hats, but never felt quite as good as I did with my hair.

At that time, I was getting chemo on weeks two and three of the five-week treatment. Because of that experience, I can understand why my hair was the last thing I had to worry about. I had to be strapped to a kind of fanny pack for a week at a time, twenty-four hours a day for five days. There was a pump inside which constantly fed the medicine into my port. It had a kind of silent pumping sound, if that makes sense. I slept with it, exercised with it, removed it carefully, still plugged into the port but out of the way to take a shower. Yes, a lot of extra work, time, and care. It was an annoyance to be sure, but I managed.

What was really hard, though, was taking the pink injections at the beginning of those two weeks. I have never seen a bigger syringe, and it was filled with a pink solution that did not remind me of bubble gum. It took a while to inject the whole syringe and then get the fanny pack situated. The best thing about it was that my other daughter, Catherine, was there. She is the perfect caregiver, encouraging without overdoing it. I didn't know it at the time, but she was texting the progress of the procedure to my best friend, Pam, to keep her updated. She had so many ways of helping behind the scenes to benefit me, like the wipes, swabs, and touches, or the coffee she made in the morning – they all contributed to my comfort, and I will always be grateful.

Sitting in that chair to receive the chemo was an experience in itself. First you have to weigh in. My weight dropped almost ten pounds, down to 110. There was a double reaction in me. First: "Oh, I am skinny for once." The second was shock that I was so thin. The other thing is that the rows of chairs with patients receiving their chemo from metal poles reminded me of a cemetery. Each chair, usually draped in a white blanket with a pale-faced patient, all in neat little rows, looked like cemetery markers. I had to get another image as fast as possible because I was in one of those chairs and did not like the thought of being in a grave.

I honestly think some of those people felt that way. As I write this, I still feel what I felt then—a sense of grave depression and sadness. The whole picture seemed so surreal. And when I thought about its purpose, to save people from death, I just had to control those thoughts and focus on thoughts of healing instead. I have seen television shows where the fictional characters meet up during their chemo sessions with what becomes a significant other. Somehow, that is hard for me to believe. I think that just concentrating on surviving is all one can think about while receiving chemo. Some are anticipating an operation, and for others it is almost more than enough just to maintain being alive while possibly, at the same time, feeling the effects of radiation.

I still am haunted by the chemo experience, although I did not have any vomiting. I did get terrible mouth sores, though, and had trouble swallowing. Perhaps that is why it was so difficult to eat. Nothing had any taste. Eating was an extreme effort. I used sponge swabs for a toothbrush. There was nothing really happy about that experience, even when I had my last round, and they rang a bell, a tradition for anyone on the last day of chemo. (I should add that my friend has just finished her chemo treatment. I asked her about the bell ringing ceremony, and she said it was a good one for her, a triumph of sorts, and she cried tears of relief.) I remember my last day of chemo, and the picture they took of me with my daughter standing right next to me was not one of joy. It was one of relief and finality for that phase being over.

Maybe it was because I did not visualize that tube coming from the metal stand and into my body as one of supply that the experience was unpleasant to say the least. I just never had the thought at the time that the blood of Jesus—His love—was pouring into me, saving me, and renewing me. I can see it now, but certainly not at the time. And that was the reason I had my one and only real breakdown, tears of fear streaming out of me. That was the time two months later when I was anticipating the biopsy procedure. I was in the midst of making an egg casserole for Christmas brunch and just broke down. "I don't know how I could hear I still have more chemo to go through," I confessed to Pam. "I just don't know if I can do it." That was the only time I even felt close to giving up. She reassured me that I would have the strength, that God would provide whatever strength and hope necessary. She reminded me that my relationship was with Jesus, not with an injection of some medicine to kill my cancer. Her words renewed my spirit because she offered me the words of life, not death. I was very grateful. I was renewed.

The bright spot in this whole ordeal happened sometime during the process. As I said, my daughter was staying with me a lot of the time. That night she was in the bathroom a very long time. I asked if she were ok.

"Sure, Mom," she said. "I was just buzzing my hair. It was getting long." Catherine had a bald head by choice for years before my cancer. My friend, Pam, was there and suggested maybe I would like mine shaved.

Without much thought I said, "Sure." Buzz, buzz, away went the last limp little pieces falling on the floor. And then I looked into the mirror and saw a new me. I was excited. I really liked it. I was transformed. What was turned over to God became one of the greatest miracles in my healing. I liked how I looked. It made me feel so much better. It was certainly a turning point—a reminder that good can come out of something so bad.

Today, I have a very short haircut, not quite shaved. And, sure enough, people come up to me to admire my hair! Who would have thought? The answer to that question is God, who always has the answer, and it is always good because He is.

Two Disturbing Questions with the Same Answer

My daughter asked the first. "Mom, what are you going to write about for people who do not have the money you do to pay for help when they are sick?"

I didn't have an immediate, practical answer because I did have help. Sue was here every day to walk Molly, take me to the doctor appointments, shop at the grocery store, pick up medicine, and run countless other errands. Catherine went on to describe other people's situations. "Mom, some people have to take the bus. They don't have the money to rent or buy a scooter. They don't have enough help during the night to give them the pills they need on time." Yes, I have thought about all of that. My first reaction was that God takes care of these things. I have had lots of experience with that when I did not have the money. He somehow always provided.

But I kept thinking about it. And then the situation of an elderly, modern-day missionary came to mind. He was outside of the meeting hall and related how he was going to go back to South Africa to help his son-in-law take Bibles into the Sudan. My immediate reaction was to question him about how he was going to finance such a trip.

"Bill, where will you get the money?" I asked. Then I realized what I had asked of a man of such a history of faith, and I became embarrassed. I looked him in the eye and answered the question myself. "You just trust God," I said, because I knew he had been behind the Iron Curtain with Bibles and was underground for months, evangelizing when each moment could have been his last. He could have been arrested, sent to a Russian prison, or worse, and there he was telling me his vision because of his faith in the Divine Provision. His experience had built his faith into a non-compromising place of belief. I will never forget that moment because it increased my faith. He was so certain.

Yes, that experience meant that I, too, and others, could depend on God for money to supply our needs. There is more to my answer, however. It comes to my mind that we have to *ask*. Not only of God, but of those around us. I believe there is always an answer. God will provide someone there to help. But we have to ask. We have to believe that we are worth it—that we do not have to put up false pretenses that we are sufficient in ourselves. I have to believe that someone will be there to answer the need, even if it would mean borrowing money for a taxi, or asking someone to make me a meal, or call when I need to take my meds. I have to believe that the goodness in people goes farther than how much I can pay.

When Sue asked me if she could do anything to help me that day, she did not stop the car to negotiate a contract about how much I would pay her an hour. She was simply a neighbor who recognized distress and offered to do something about it. If I had stopped to think about how much it would cost in advance of ASKING, I would have missed the joy of God sending me an angel out of nowhere to help me. I really believe that Sue would have helped me even if I did not have one cent to pay her. And when I stop to really think about it, I repaid her more in friendship than one million dollars would have given her. No one in my mind had ever given her enough credit for being the loving, giving person she is, and that assignment was a no-brainer for me. It is easy for me to see the good in others and to make it known. What we both got out of the arrangement was more than any money could buy. I also got a best friend who was formerly a stranger. And you ask if I believe in angels? The answer is a resounding, "YES."

The second question came up at Book Club today. We had read a book where the young character had sacrificed his college scholarship to stay home to take care of an alcoholic dad. He had been abandoned by his mom early in his life and ended up being killed by someone he was trying to save. His life was one of complete self-sacrifice. So, the question was: "Who was the victim in the novel?"

It seemed obvious it was him. He spent his short life trying to rescue others and came to a tragic end. Sad. Very sad. However, I had another thought. My question to our group was, "Is it a good thing to try to rescue someone?" We really thought about it. He could have made entirely different choices. Not one of the people he was struggling to help had actually asked him for help, nor had he asked if they wanted it. He took it upon himself to sacrifice his life for people who were not even interested in helping themselves. He was rescuing, not helping. I am sure his intentions were sincere and generous. He probably even thought he was doing the right and loving thing. The problem was he did not practice Christ's message of abundance rather than sacrifice. He never asked.

That discussion took me to Jesus and His healing ministry. He was always asked before He healed anyone. He did not impose His healing. He waited for the question, "Are You willing to heal me?"

What a lesson! And then, of course, I thought of the Bible verse that tells us to keep knocking and asking our Heavenly Father, and He will answer because that is His Word, and He cannot break His promise.

> Keep on asking and it will be given you; keep on seeking and you will find; keep on knocking [reverently] and [the door] will be opened to you.

> For everyone who keeps on asking receives; and he who keeps on seeking finds; and to him who keeps on knocking, [the door] will be opened. (Matthew 7:7-8 TELB)

It always delights me when I recognize that God is ahead of me with His answers. All I have to do is ASK!

He even repeats the message in Luke 11:10 in case we didn't get it before!

> For everyone who asks and keeps on asking receives; and he who seeks and keeps on seeking finds; and to him who knocks and keeps on knocking, the door shall be opened. (TELB)

View from the Floor

It was a very familiar place on the carpeted floor by the kitchen right outside my bedroom. That was where I lay on my back each morning to stretch, so I could at least relieve some of my pain from my back. I had to be careful because sometimes the "fanny pack" with the chemo was attached to my waist. I did not want to disconnect the tube to the port or roll over on the pack.

Each morning I could see the tree from the floor through the window. I wondered if it might be nice to have a hummingbird feeder out there. It would be fun and/or distracting, at least, to watch the birds and maybe take my mind off some of my pain. Sure enough, I had the thought, and the garage door opened; Sue walked in with my dog, Molly, barking, of course, so happy to be with her walker.

"Sue," I asked, "do you think you could hang a feeder on that tree?"

"Sure," was her reply, and by that afternoon, it was there for the next morning routine.

I loved seeing the birds. The problem was that the birds gobbled up the liquid, and I couldn't walk out there to change the feeder. But—you guessed it—Sue bought the mix and got it up there without a problem for my delight. Those hummingbirds teach a lot of lessons. That you can move and yet be still was one of them. I related it to myself. I could move in my mind with visions of healing while perfectly still on the floor. "The day will come," I thought.

And it did. I was better, able to stand a little, and I thought about my filling the feeder myself. But then the fear set in. "Oh, no," I thought.

"I won't be able to reach it up in the tree. It is so high." So, of course, I asked Sue if she could do it once again. She said, "I think you can reach it yourself." I trust her, so out I went. I stood in front of the tree, stretched out my arm, and was surprised that the feeder was directly in front of me. I didn't even have to stand on tiptoes. It was in perfect eye view, not up high and unreachable at all.

That was a huge lesson. What I had thought was way beyond my reach was right in front of me. All I had to do was reach. From the floor it looked impossible, but after the treatment and healing and surgery, it was easy. And that is what I always think about. What seems so difficult can become easy with faith in the God Who promises that all things are possible with Him. "But Jesus looked at them and said, 'With men this is impossible, but all things are possible with God.'" (Matthew 19:26 TELB)

The limited "view from the floor" became a symbol of what I thought I could not do. I attribute it to the mindset of illness. For so long, I could not do the ordinary things I had spent 76 years doing with ease. So, when I had something to do or to be done, I had to think of a way to get it done or how to get the help to get it done. That way of thinking becomes a kind of "I can't" mentality, whereas before I had an "I can do it myself" mentality. It is a mindset I wasn't really aware of until the bird feeder incident, but there were others. I can see now that it has taken time for me to completely come out of the "patient state of mind."

An example of this is when we went to Disney after the cancer and operation. We got to the hotel room, and I couldn't get the remote to work quickly, so I asked my nephew (who had his hands full of baggage) to please check it out. He was stunned that his aunt—who was, in his mind, so competent and capable—would interrupt him to fix a remote that she could ordinarily handle for herself in a nanosecond. He seemed rude to me at the time, like it was a huge inconvenience to stop to fix the TV. I realized later, however, that he had never seen me needy, especially about something so easy to remedy. I had to think about it and came up with the answer for myself. I had been so used to needing help that it had become a habit. I got so used to asking for help that I began to do it routinely, even when not needed. It was a lesson in what I call coming out of the "patient forever" comfort zone.

That was a small thing, but, nonetheless, another message that I could be more independent. My body was able; I had to get my mind to catch up. For so long the fear and the pain were my reality. Now the freedom without it needed expression.

Despite these reminders, I ultimately had to be jolted out of being taken care of. It happened at the physical therapy office where I had been going for over a year. My physical therapist was the best, encouraging me through the back problem and the cancer ordeal and then the surgery. She had taught me exercises to perform at each stage of my healing. I love her and respect her for knowing just what would be most helpful for me. And then the day came when it was over. Abruptly. I was making several more appointments when she suggested that maybe other patients needed her time. Because we live in Arizona, many of her patients were on their way here from the north for warmer weather. I never thought that I was hoarding her time—I was shocked to think that she might think I was greedy, needing more of her time than necessary. I was offended at first; it felt like being kicked out. And then the revelation came. It was her way of setting me free. It was the bird feeder all over again: not unattainable, but right there in the moment. It was over. I was well.

I still thank her for her directness and for setting me free. I have had other very anxious moments as the time of the treatment gets farther and farther into the past. However, recognizing the fact that the mind can decide its reality, that I am sick or healed, was a huge factor in my inner peace and my continued physical healing.

We are familiar with the Scripture that tells us to call those things that be not as though they were. I did that, but needed help from the Holy Spirit to remind me that it worked! I had called my healing into being but needed more of His help to recognize it!

I am reminded of the verses in Romans 4:20-21 which say: "He [Abraham] staggered not at the promise of God through unbelief; but was strong in faith, giving glory to God; And being fully persuaded that, what he had promised, he was able also to perform." (KJV) I thank God that He did not let me "stagger" under the weight of the ordeal but lifted me up and pursued me with His love during the whole time it took (and takes) to be well.

Why God? Why?

Her name is Carolyn. She is one of the smartest, wisest, and holiest women I know. When I was searching for a purpose and didn't know what to do with my time, my friend, Pam, suggested that I go visit Carolyn, who lives around the corner and down the block. With the pain in my leg at the time, and in a mental state of non-focus, I put it off. Then at Christmas something something prompted me to call and wish her a Merry Christmas. She answered, and I could tell she was in distress. She had suffered a broken bone which put her on bedrest for eight weeks, having to have complete care. The expense was enormous.

"Why, God? Why?" With enough on my plate to deal with and healing from cancer, I put Carolyn and her problems in the background. It was months later, after my back surgery and all my cancer treatments, that I was at a prayer meeting, and one of my friends asked if someone would volunteer to read to Carolyn. Her sight was getting worse and worse. She could barely see, and Mary, who visited her and read to her each Sunday, was going to be out of town. Something deep within me knew that I was the one to volunteer. And I did.

Sometimes a call from God can come, and answering it can be delayed. Such was the case with Carolyn. Months had gone by before my weekly visits started. We have since become the best of friends. Yet each time I am there and then have to leave, there is a heaviness around my heart. I want her to be able to see. She is eighty-five and has had a remarkable life. She is a published writer, a travel expert, and her house is filled with books that she can no longer read. Still, she knows where they are and remembers what they said. She told me that before her eyesight got bad, she went to the library twice a week and took out ten books at a time. She called a library a "cathedral of ideas." And yet, there she sits in a chair, well-worn with her slight body impression, not able to read. "Why, God? Why?"

One day, as it is each time I visit, she was very excited to tell me that I was to write this book. She had taught writing and, therefore, had an exact plan for me. I was to get ten folders, title each one with an idea, write about that idea, and then put that writing in the folder. It would be later that I would sort them, get chapters, and get some editing. She stirred something deep within me because I had always thought I would write. "You must encourage others who are going through cancer," she said with an urgency I could not ignore. It was a good idea, I thought, but I had the Christmas season approaching and lots and lots of promises to fulfill. Writing takes time. It takes a dedication. And yet I felt compelled to start.

One day she showed me a poster she had made years before. She could see enough to find it in the house. We stood in front of a collage of pictures of waterfalls. Each one was cut from a magazine and was not glued too tightly. She asked me which one I wanted. I picked one which showed water falling over rugged rocks, symbolizing to me how the flow of His grace soothes the rough times we endure. That was the point, she explained. Waterfalls to her were the representation of God's wonderful, refreshing, flowing grace. She would visualize herself standing under the falls with her hands outstretched while receiving His abundant love. That vision sustained her. That vision she told me would inspire me to write as I saw His words flow through me to lift someone else's heart. I love Carolyn.

And so, gradually, I am getting an answer to "Why, God? Why?" Carolyn can see beyond sight. She has often told me that because she is housebound, she has more ministry than ever before. Besides her care-givers, who come four times a week, she has neighbors and friends drop-ping by. She can teach without sight and even in silence because just coming into her house and seeing how she is managing and hearing her talk about Him is so uplifting. Despite this, she is also very real. There are days she tells me that the darkness is growing. And sometimes she has anxiety attacks, calmed only by her belief in His presence and her keen memory of Scripture. When she has an idea, and she is alone, she writes it down on a piece of paper the best she can in big print with a Sharpie and saves it for one of us to read. Her spirit is what is alive. Her spirit is stronger each time I visit. Her spirit gives me hope. She told me lately that while her eyes may be closing, the eyes of her heart are wide open.

Today I read the following in Proverbs 19:21: "There are many devices in a man's heart; nevertheless the counsel of the Lord, that shall stand." (KJV) What that means to me is that we have our plans, but it is God's purpose that will be carried out. That is the answer to "Why, God? Why?" for me today. I see His purpose for Carolyn very clearly. If only just that she is there for me. She has read my heart and given me purpose, fulfilling my dream to write that I had never actualized until now. It took her, the subject of cancer, and my (what she calls) "radical hope" to make it happen.

THE PILLAR

There are stories and images that last a lifetime. One of those was of a primitive, nomadic tribe that had a pole which they took from place to place. The pole was always placed in the center of the community around which all the activities took place. It was a center, a symbol that all was well and that the people were planted exactly where they were meant to be for that time. One time, for an unknown reason, the pole broke. It lay in pieces on the ground. When the people realized what had happened, they all lay down on the ground and died.

That story had a huge impact on me. I realized over my lifetime that certain beliefs, events, and people around which I centered my well-being were vital to my happiness, and maybe even my survival. Yes, there were times of devastation, like going through the divorce when it felt like the center of my existence—my identity as a wife—was shattered. The pole had broken. However, just knowing the story I realized that I had to get a new pole in my consciousness. I had to hold on to something else to give me strength. Over the years, that took the form of new beliefs, a stronger faith, and people in my life to support all of it.

That person in my life is my best friend, Pam. She is not only the "pole" for me, but for our whole family. We met at the high school where we both taught. I was so unhappy with my life and in search of something, anything, to fill up the place of pain in my life with peace. I watched how she lived her life and especially how she thought. At the time, she was researching and studying the brain—how the left brain and the right brain could work together to give a bigger picture of reality, actualize our biotic potential, and bring abundance. We started working together when her book was published. I had finally found a way, with her instruction, to know that I could think about the way I think. I could be in control of my thoughts and direct them to see that God was always giving me more abundance from every situation if I chose to think it that way. Her favorite Scripture is John 10:10: "...I came that they may have and enjoy life, and have it in abundance (to the full, till it overflows)." (TELB).

One of the main tenets in her teaching is that we are never victims. We cannot be victims of anything nor anybody. The idea is that by seeing myself as a conqueror, I am opening myself to a new way of seeing something and allowing something greater than what seems to be. The Bible says it this way in Romans 8:31: "What shall we then say to these things? If God be for us, who can be against us?" (KJV)

As friends and colleagues, we applied that message to so many incidents in our lives. Retiring from teaching, moving to Arizona, and then experiencing the sudden death of her husband, we had to commit to something so strong and firm and immoveable. She was a "pillar," planted firmly in the belief that God was in charge and something better would be coming. She never wavered. There were certainly other challenges, and somehow with her commitment to the truth she knew and the faith she professed, things became better and better. Grief was swallowed up by attention to the Holy Spirit giving direction for the future. She listens to His direction and follows His lead.

That direction brought us a new career in real estate; we enjoyed lots of success and shared a great sense of purpose. She was the inspiration. She was also the center for a new family, one including me, of course, and including her son, Dane, his wife, Tanya, and her parents, Nick and Darla. Pam always knew that we could form a village to support and care for one another. Little by little, over twenty years, that has brought us to a design/building team to construct a multi-generational home for us on property that we had purchased years before.

And were there ever struggles. Her vision is so clear and precise it reminds me of the book of Leviticus, of all things. Every order God gives in that book is extremely specific. That is Pam. She is the pillar, planted in the knowing that the Holy Spirit is the One who leads and guides us. Getting the messages can take time, meditation, and patience. The difficult part comes when she knows something while others cannot see nor understand it. Her frustration must be enormous. Maybe in the story of the pole, it broke because it was not tended to, not given the attention it needed. I have seen Pam stressed, but unlike the story, she never quit and never broke. I believe it is because she believes in His strength, not her own.

So where was my best friend when I was diagnosed? What was she experiencing when she saw me on the floor in such great pain? She was right there with the knowing that I would be ok. How did she know that? Because she believes, like I said before, that everything happens for more. That belief and our faith in it caused her to never lose faith in me and my healing. She was the pillar I have come to love over the years because she cannot compromise her belief in more. She was the pole of knowing—just knowing, never overreacting—that I needed to heal. I needed to *know* that her trust and faith in God was permanent and non-bending. That was the strength Pam gave to me. I could look at her and know I would not die. I would not fall down because she would not break. Of course, if she had a weak moment, as we all do, I knew she would regain her strength and that she would come back stronger than before.

I must add that she was wonderful with the doctors. Her razor-sharp mind asked the right questions while sometimes I would be in a fog. My oncologist often observed that I was so blessed to have a friend like Pam. She is the one who suggested that my daughter come right away to give me help. She was the one who posted the calendar on the kitchen wall so I could mark off each day of radiation when it was over. She was the one who suggested I take sixty grams of protein each day and keep track of those grams on a tablet. All those suggestions were of a great help, especially taking the protein *and* making me keep track of it. I had asked the doctor how long it would take for me to recover my energy after the treatment. He told us about six months to a year. By taking the protein, my energy was restored very quickly. I was able to have surgery a few months later.

She also had me walk a little at a time. "Walk past two houses and then rest and come home." Because of the specific assignment, I was less afraid of overdoing. I would do that and then go a little farther each day. Pam is very accurate. I trust her accurate instructions. Her belief and mine is if our left brains have a task, like counting the number of protein grams or the number of steps I took, then the right brain was free to do what it was supposed to do, to help heal my body. Worry or stress over healing would impede that process. A clear plan was not only very reassuring; it insured that I made progress.

Pam's function in my life is not to give sympathetic looks or give a pity party. She holds up the truth for me. I see myself in her, someone who believes in possibility. I like the verse in the Bible which says that a friend is closer than a brother. She is that friend. "...but there is a friend who sticks closer than a brother." (Proverbs 18:24 TELB)

Yes, she is a pillar, a pillar of strength because her life breath is His, and she knows it and lives it. I often think that God must REALLY love me to have given me such a friend.

THE GLASS CROSS IN THE CHINA CABINET

Carolyn emphasized that I write about forgiveness. I had a hard time with it because I did not feel there was anyone with whom I held a grudge or felt had offended me that I had not already addressed in my life. I was wrong, and looking at each example and confronting it has given me a peace I had not known I was missing.

The first was a very good friend, and I mean a *very* good friend. She had sent me a fabulous, unexpected birthday present. It was a floral piece loaded with white flowers with a glass cross in the middle. It was totally unexpected and lavish. Whenever I think of the word "lavish," I think of 1 John 3:1. *The King James Version* puts it this way: "Behold, what manner of love the Father hath bestowed upon us, that we should be called the sons of God...." In other words, His calling us "sons" is pretty lavish! I love that word, "lavish." It reminds me of a magnitude of beauty, joy, abundance, and even extravagance. And that is how I felt about my birthday gift—lavished and loved.

The mistake I made was assigning my feelings to that gift. Remember, it had a glass cross in the center of it. Instead of focusing that only God can "lavish" me, I had attributed it to a friend and the expectations that went with it. So, when I told her I had cancer, I expected to be "lavished" with well-wishes, calls, and lots of attention. None of it came except for what felt like a brief "hope you are doing well." I really felt hurt, disappointed, and dispirited. Why? Because my expectations were on her, rather than on the God of my supply.

I placed the cross in the china cabinet where I saw it each morning while on the floor doing my exercises. One time I thought I would just give it to a friend so I wouldn't be reminded of my hurt. That didn't happen. Little by little the pain just dissipated, and instead of feeling hurt, I started to see what that cross meant. It meant that He had died for me. That He took all my sufferings and pain and gave me the promise of health and healing. Little by little I saw the beauty of the cross. I saw His hurt, His humiliation, His suffering, and I knew He did it all for me. I took all the small, little expectations I had projected on my friend and realized I was the one in the wrong. I was not being her friend by thinking that she had rejected me. Gradually, I began to realize that maybe she loved me so much, she couldn't bear the thought of my suffering. My understanding of how others respond to a friend's suffering may not be the way I think I would. Slowly the cross became a comfort to me. It not only told me that He was my Savior, but that someone loved me so much, she lavished her love on me. It was my job to remember, to hold the love, to keep the joy of the gift and to give up any other thought of hurt. It was to **give** myself another way to see the whole situation.

And I did. Complete peace about the situation enveloped my heart. Only later did I discover that she had undergone serious surgery at the same time as my chemo and radiation. She had been through months of pain, surgery, and rehab without my knowing it. Needless to say, in that condition, she was unable to reach out to me. Perhaps she did not want to further burden me with the knowledge of what she was enduring. What a lesson.

Today the cross in the cupboard is a daily reminder of where my focus ought to be—on Him, the One Who took it all. My focus and love are also on the Holy Spirit, Who gave me the revelation to refocus on His love, rather than what I expected I needed from others. Oh, how grateful I am. I am lavished with His love!

There was another incident where I overreacted with anxiety and hurt and anger. It happened a few days before the operation. It seemed that I was overlooked in a celebration that I felt I had the right to be part of. It was a part of my legacy, so I thought.

Usually, I don't need credit for something the Holy Spirit inspires me to say or do. In fact, I believe His ideas are gifts and opportunities to give Him the glory. Well, in the case I have written about, I wasn't even able to do that. Because it happened right before the operation, I think the anxiety was magnified due to the fear that I could die during that surgery. I wanted my legacy to be "an inspirer of ideas," at least that is what I had thought, and it would not happen in the way I thought it should.

That is when I seriously thought about "legacy." I had to redefine what it would be for me—one of character, not accomplishment. I struggled about it, finally realizing that who I am is more important than the things I accomplished in my life. It is who we are in the process, always giving the thanks and recognition to the God Who gives us the strength, the purpose and the desire in the first place.

Forgiveness. Forgiveness means asking God to give me a different way of looking at things through His eyes. To see how He loves me. To see that there is no other way but to see how He sees the "other," the one who seemed to give the offense. He would see them with eyes and a heart of love. Being hurt is FOR GIVING me the opportunity to do the same.

A Hand in the Night from Unexpected Places

V isitations, manifestations, and demonstrations. Yes, her reaching out to me in the night with a gentle voice, saying, "Mom, it is time to take your medicine," was an example of all three. Jerry Saville had introduced that trio of words some time back, and I have never forgotten them. In fact, I have grown to expect all three and hear myself acknowledging them when I feel or see what I think is a direct example of God's love.

There it was in the middle of the night, and I was being ministered by a daughter who one year before had been in St. Thomas during the hurricanes with no money, a seven-year old daughter, and a problem with drinking. And there she was in Arizona, sober, loving, and giving me the kind of emotional and physical attention that I so longed for and needed. I felt so loved.

What was better about the situation with Catherine coming from California was the fact that she showed such a heart of love and compassion. The healing for me was that all the mistakes I had made during her childhood were washed away; her heart was one of pure love. No matter what the past shadowed, or what memories of trouble, they were all washed in that one act of her hand in the middle of the night and her sweet voice saying, "Mom, it is time to take your pills."

I think that one of the most important reasons I am healed is gratitude for every little and big act of kindness extended to me. Each instance of someone reaching out with any kind of help all added up to an amazing gift. Recognizing those kindnesses was the key. Receiving them, taking them in, and knowing that the love of God was being given to me through their hands was the key.

There were many examples of His love extended through doctors, nurses, neighbors, and friends. I received many cards promising prayers and love. I have come to believe that everyone of us reaching out and receiving love and kindness is what is meant by "the Body of Christ."

I want to say more about Catherine. I remember that I had an urge to ask her to come from California. I needed her but did not acknowledge it. Pam, however, read my heart on the way home from the doctor's office very early on—even before the treatment started. She suggested that I call Catherine and ask her to come right away. I agreed immediately. I am so grateful to Pam; she read my heart during my whole journey. It is one of my life's greatest blessings. Catherine did come right away. Catherine was familiar with cancer. She had taken care of her sister-in-law, whom she had kept alive for many years longer than expected. She has the gift of ministering angels.

Catherine is the kind of person who does something without being asked. The coffee is made. Swabs were ordered and in the bathroom. She texted Pam at every appointment to update her on my chemo injections. She ordered audio books and put them on my phone. She made the most incredible things in the Instapot. She shared her presence with me over many visits. I felt so loved. I cried a bit each time she left and couldn't wait for her to return.

Looking back, I realize that being treated with so much medication and radiation, and then having the back surgery a few months later, put me into a state of weakness, a certain kind of surrender that I had not experienced before. My identity had shifted in subtle but real ways, from one of strength to one of weakness. I needed all the help I could get! My surrender to the healing was magnified greatly by the gratitude I felt and expressed nonstop. Interestingly enough, the surrender and gratitude ended up giving me a stronger identity than I could ever have imagined.

One of the Bible verses I saw years ago that filed in my heart is the one in Isaiah 41:13, which says, "For I the LORD thy God will hold thy right hand, saying unto thee, Fear not; I will help thee." (KJV) He surely has kept His promise.

The other verse that certainly applies to so many of the healings I received is in Jeremiah 32:17: "Alas, Lord God! You have made the heavens and the earth by Your great power and by Your outstretched arm! There is nothing too hard or too wonderful for You." (TELB)

MUSIC IN THE BACKGROUND

About seven years before my cancer journey, I had accepted the responsibility of my oldest sister's life. She had become extremely ill with signs of dementia. I moved her to Arizona and settled her in an assisted living home. Usually after a visit I feel sad about her being there while I am free to leave. It also made me sad to see a resident with coat and purse, determined that her daughter was on her way to take her home. The truth, of course, is that neither she nor my sister can ever leave to live on their own. Both have debilitating forms of dementia.

But that day when I left, I was happy, not sad. What was different? I had left the six residents sitting around the dining table, and they were smiling. Why? Loud and wonderful music was playing in the background, so loud an orchestra could have been in the same room. Its sound drowned out any silence that would normally have prevailed, due to all six being incapable of conversing logically with each other. Whatever their minds were thinking or processing usually didn't make sense. But that day with the music, everyone was communicating a sense of happiness. It was palpable. The language of the music permeated the heart of the table, and any indecipherable communication was drowned in glorious music that replaced any negative thought or feeling with joy and well-being.

That incident and my unusual uplifted reaction upon leaving made me think of how similar the effect of the music was to the effect I receive when praying in tongues. The utterances of my tongue make no sense to me at all. However, I find myself praying in tongues in my head or out loud almost constantly. And I certainly did while going through cancer.

It all started at a Believer's Voice of Victory meeting in Fort Worth, years and years ago. I had heard of praying in tongues. An announcer invited those of us who wanted to learn more to go to a separate room. I wasn't sure, but a friend encouraged me, and I decided I had nothing to lose. I am not sure exactly what they said, but I was surprised that I had a unique language. What surprised me was that I had used that same language in the classroom many times as a kind of "getting the students' attention" technique. When they needed to settle down, I would loudly mutter sounds that seemed like the mimic of my dad's German. Never until later did I realize that I was probably praying in tongues right there in a public high school. Whenever I used that expression of "muttering," it brought my students to immediate attention. Now I know why.

What is praying in tongues to me, and why do I think it was so helpful during the chemo, the radiation, the pain, and the waiting? My answer is that it establishes a private and intimate conversation with God. Only He and the Holy Spirit really know what I need and what I want. I feel like He is translating my deepest thoughts—that He is transforming my deepest fears into faith. That is what it really takes to pray in the Spirit: faith. I have to surrender an agenda of thoughts and submit to what the Holy Spirit is directing.

This morning I was awakened by pain all over my body. It was really quite unusual because I sleep very well. I wondered about the timing of such an onslaught of pain. It certainly could have been a distraction from writing this chapter this morning, which had been my goal. Could it be that the power of praying in tongues is so threatening to the devil that he put a huge distraction in my body? Like, "Why do you think you can write about the power of healing when you are having pain?" The devil is a liar and a thief, as it says in John 10:10. Right next to those words are the ones which promise life and the enjoyment of it. Jesus said He came "that they may have and enjoy life, and have it in abundance (to the full, till it overflows)." (TELB)

Needless to say, my spirit was able to see my discomfort this morning as a distraction. I am calling into being a pain free and youthful body and am fully convinced that I am to write this chapter.

Back to music and an unfamiliar language. One of the Bible verses I love the most is the one which says we can pray in a language "too deep for words." That promise helped me so much because I did not know of any way to be able to endure cancer, back surgery, and all the intrusion into a normal life they presented. My escape was to picture myself walking free of cancer, wearing new denim farmer's overalls. I had seen them on a lady in a store months before, and I loved the look. Lying on the floor, I pictured myself that way. But to get there from the floor to a fashion presentation took a lot of faith. I had a vision as suggested in Romans 8:25 which says to hope for what we cannot see, but I needed assurance that I was doing something to get it. And that is when I prayed in the Spirit, in "groanings too deep for words." I was believing that God would love the idea, too, and that He was preparing my body to be able to stand up, walk, and strut in that new outfit. I was emotional about it. I even ordered the denim and hung it right in front of my closet to remind me of my vision. I renewed my faith with the following, found in Romans 8:25-26.

> But if we hope for what is still unseen by us, we wait for it with patience and composure. So too, the [Holy] Spirit comes to our aid and bears us up in our weakness; for we do not know what prayer to offer nor how to offer it worthily as we ought, but the Spirit Himself goes to meet our supplication and pleads in our behalf with unspeakable yearnings and groaning too deep for utterance. (TELB)

What a fabulous God we serve, to provide us with the commandment to "speak to the mountain" and then provide us with the means to do so when we cannot figure out how. I am in awe of His generosity.

About four months later, I put on the denim overalls and walked to a brunch with only the assistance of Tanya's arm. It meant so much to me that it was Tanya who assisted me. She is the one who two years before had prayed for my health, way before the back pain and cancer. She couldn't have known what was going to happen. I believe it was the Holy Spirit's plan right then to unite us in a relationship of faith and prayer that helped me to heal. He already had the plan for how her prayer was to come true!

My new "look" brought me more joy than the compliments I received. I knew it was the Holy Spirit and the Father's plan to get me into that place of joy. And my secret language provided me with an intimate reassurance of how He listens and answers prayer.

I am often asked, "How do you learn to pray that language?" I suggest starting with a desire for it and then asking the Holy Spirit how to do it. I also recommend starting with the repetition of "AAA, BBB, CCC, DDD...." That is a good way to get started. It overcomes wondering how to do it. It shuts down the left brain, allowing the Spirit to take over, and He does.

We say something is "beyond words" when in a state of awe, disbelief, shock, or fear. When that happens, the Holy Spirit can step right in and take whatever the emotion and pray it out to bring peace and much better understanding. He offers so much; all we have to do is receive.

Instead of all the background noise in our lives, instead of the chatter in our heads, we can turn to the "music" of His language, knowing that it is on its way to bringing great results. Romans 8:27-28 makes the promise.

> And He Who searches the hearts of men knows what is in the mind of the [Holy] Spirit [what His intent is], because the Spirit intercedes and pleads [before God] in behalf of the saints according to and in harmony with God's will. We are assured and know [that God being a partner in their labor] all things work together and are [fitting into a plan] for good to and for those who love God and are called according to [His] design and purpose. (TELB)

What a promise!

MAKING SURE

It was Christmas morning. Pam came over to check on the egg casserole we were going to take to brunch. That was the day I broke down. The next day, the day after Christmas, was my scheduled appointment for the biopsy. The results would show if there were any evidence of the cancer left. I didn't realize how much stress I was feeling. It was the day that Christ was born, and all I could think about was, "What if they tell me I still have cancer left in my body?" I told Pam about my fear. It was the first time I had ever admitted to myself or anyone that I was afraid that the treatment didn't work. I had faced the deepest fear in me, one I didn't even realize I had.

That reminds me of the time in the Bible when the Israelites were overcome with a plague. They had spoken against God and Moses, and the Lord sent fiery serpents among them which bit them and even killed some. Then the people begged Moses to ask God for help. They also repented of their sins. The Bible tells us that Moses then "prayed for the people." The first thing he did was pray. An all-forgiving God sent the answer, and a very interesting one in my opinion. He asked Moses to make a bronze serpent, place it on a pole, and tell the people who were bitten to look at it. And "...when he looks at it, [he] shall live."

> And Moses made a serpent of bronze and put it on
> a pole, and if a serpent had bitten any man, when he
> looked to the serpent of bronze [attentively, expectantly,

with a steady and absorbing gaze], he lived. (Numbers 21: 8-9 TELB)

This incident tells me so many things. When I broke down to confess my fear to Pam that morning, I was facing my fear. I told her that I did not think I could ever go through the experience of getting chemo again. I looked that cancer, that serpent, right in the eye. By confessing my fear, she could lift me up with words of truth. "You absolutely could go through it again if you have to. You have the strength. You have the determination. You have proven it." Yes, I had. What she did was point me to look at Jesus on the cross, rather than at a serpent on a pole. She reminded me that He had died to make me whole, not just in spirit but also in body. I was reassured. I enjoyed the day. I then prepared for the procedure the next day.

And sure enough, when we had to leave the next morning, it was cloudy and cold. When I arrived at the office, I was the only one in the waiting room. It was the day after Christmas, and most people did not want to fast on Christmas Day in order to prepare for colonoscopies. Since I was having a biopsy, I only had to fast past midnight.

Sue left to park the car, and then the wait began. Another wait; more anxiety. I was hungry after fasting that morning, and I prayed for an outcome that would be: "No cancer." I was taken to pre-op, put on the gurney, hooked up to the IV after two punctures and given a lukewarm blanket before they drew the curtain around me, shutting me off from the huge room. I could only hear a patient next to me. We were the only ones there in the post-holiday surgery section. My thought was that since we were the only ones there, the wait would not be long. All was ok for a while. A nurse took me to the bathroom with IV attached. I was ready. But then the wait began again. And the wait did not stop. I could hear nurses outside the curtains talking about the wonderful roast they had for Christmas dinner. I started salivating. Another hour went by. Finally, after two hours, someone came to check on me, and I asked that the curtain be opened. I needed to look out of my cubbyhole. I needed to see the clock. And I still waited. Finally, someone came back to tell me that I was due for the surgery room in about forty more minutes. That helped. All that time, I was praying in the Spirit and trying to keep calm. All I can say is that without the prayer of tongues in my head, I think I would have yelled out in the loudest possible voice, "Hey! Did you forget me?" And I probably would have been terribly embarrassed.

Then a nurse came, introduced herself and put her hand on my arm. That human contact was a balm from heaven. It was SO comforting, so soothing. Amazing. I thanked her for that comfort and said it was a gift from heaven. All I knew was that the waiting was over, even though I didn't have the results. Her hand on my arm was like a sign, letting me know that I was loved and protected. There really are no words for the comfort it brought. Human touch. And it reminds me of Jesus and the storm on the sea. Jesus walked on the water to come to the disciples.

> And when the disciples saw Him walking on the sea, they were terrified and said, It is a ghost! And they screamed out with fright.
>
> But instantly He spoke to them, saying, Take courage! I AM! Stop being afraid!
>
> And Peter answered Him, Lord, if it is You, command me to come to You on the water.
>
> He said, Come! So Peter got out of the boat and walked on the water, and he came toward Jesus.
>
> But when he perceived and felt the strong wind, he was frightened, and as he began to sink, he cried out, Lord, save me [from death]!
>
> Instantly Jesus reached out His hand and caught and held him, saying to him, O you of little faith, why did you doubt?
>
> And when they got into the boat, the wind ceased. (Matthew 14:26-32 TELB)

That incident fits me perfectly. I was so scared. I tried to be brave but was having great difficulty until she reached out and put her hand on my arm. There it was: peace and reassurance.

The next thing I knew was that I was fast asleep and then woke up in the same cubbyhole. Only this time it was filled with the doctor and his good news that he did not find any more cancer. However, and there seems to always be a "however," he said I would have to have a follow up in six months. I am happy to say that the next procedure was much more peaceful because I knew in my heart FOR SURE that I was healed, and the procedure confirmed it.

I have to add a footnote here. There appeared another angel that day. He was an anesthesiologist who checked on me. I shared how happy I was about the results of the procedure but that I was still suffering from radical pain in my leg coming from the back. He came closer to the bed and shared about the successful back surgery his father-in-law had undergone. I asked for the surgeons' names and asked Sue to please write them down. With his encouragement, a whole new window of faith opened for me. I decided to investigate surgery which I had previously decided against. That window opened a world of relief because I pursued the promise and had the surgery. My pain is gone. I will be forever grateful to him for taking the time and the care of sharing hope with me.

I relaxed on the backseat of Sue's car on the way home. I was past the cancer and faced with going through back surgery. I was half rejoicing over the good news and at the same time contemplating another ordeal. Only God in His sweet way gets us through life, one moment at a time. One moment at a time is all that was possible for me. I can envision God looking down on me at that moment and smiling. He knew that "With men this is impossible, but all things are possible with God." (Matt. 19:26 TELB) And God was right!

There is another thing to add about strength. Getting through chemo and radiation takes a toll on the body, which everyone knows. However, I was able to have back surgery in February after finishing the cancer treatment just three months before. As I mentioned earlier, Pam had suggested I take sixty grams of protein a day and keep track of the number. I did. It helped to renew my strength tremendously. Praise God for His provision. I also meditated on Isaiah 40:31.

But those who wait for the Lord [who expect, look for, and hope in Him] shall change and renew their strength and power; they shall lift their wings and mount up [close to God] as eagles [mount up to the sun]; they shall run and not be weary, they shall walk and not faint or become tired. (TELB)

My strength is renewed. I can walk and run if I had to! I have the motorized scooter sitting in the garage unused until we all use it in the Disney parks. And the motorized chair has been given to a family with an impaired child. Yes, God takes care of everything!

That is clearly stated in Jeremiah 32:27. "Behold, I am the Lord, the God of all flesh; is there anything too hard for Me?" (TELB)

HELP! PLEASE! THANK YOU!

I joined a prayer group after recovering. That day we found out that our leader, Pat, had just discovered severe physical problems and needed an operation. We asked her when the operation would take place. It would be an operation on the only kidney she had left, which was connected to the ureter which was being overtaken by cancer. There I was, sitting around the table completely healed. I felt a combination of horror of what she had ahead of her and a confidence that she would be fine. Someone offered the suggestion and vision that we would be surrounding her with prayer the whole way through. We were her angels, her support group, her believers in healing. And I knew how much that kind of support meant and continues to mean to me.

Again, I thought about where I got the support to become so healed, so strong and so healthy. I have to have answers for myself and others when they ask me how I got through the cancer, then the back surgery, and then chronic itching. Today I read the story in Exodus of Moses facing a huge battle between the Israelis and Amalek. He was up on a mountain looking down on the battle. Whenever he raised his hand, the battle would favor the Israelis. When he got tired, and he did, he put his hand down, and the enemy would advance. That scene has been a part of my consciousness for a very long time, but not as clearly seen as today. There is more to the story than just friends holding up his hands, as necessary as that was.

First, Moses knew that he had the power of God in him. He could exercise his authority over his enemies because his hand held "the rod of God." How do I relate that to my life? For me the rod symbolizes the promise of God for me to triumph over my enemy, cancer. And in my case, the "rod" was the Word of God. By His "stripes [that wounded] Him we are healed and made whole." (Is 53:5 TELB) I also knew that my body was and is the Temple of the Holy Spirit, and that I had to believe He lived in me and was healing me from the inside out. So, the first step in my healing was to hold the rod of faith in my hand, in my head, in my believing, and never let go.

The next step was to allow friends to hold up my arms when I needed physical and spiritual strength. That is what Aaron and Hur did for Moses. That is what Pam and Sue did for me. But first, before Aaron and Hur held up his arms, others put a stone under him so he could sit.

> But Moses' hands were heavy and grew weary. So [the other men] took a stone and put it under him and he sat on it. Then Aaron and Hur held up his hands, one on one side and one on the other side; so his hands were steady until the setting of the sun. (Exodus 17:12 TELB)

Yes, I had to sit down. I had to sit on all I had studied about His healing power. I had to sit on all the testimonies I had read in the *The Believer's Voice of Victory* magazines over the years. I had to sit on all the memories of the times God had come through for me. I had to SIT and be still, as instructed in Psalm 46:10, where it says: "Let be and be still, and know (recognize and understand) that I am God...." (TELB) I had to sit on trusting Him with all my strength.

Once Moses sat, his friends could help him. This is an interesting point that I make time and time again. I had to accept help. The help from Pam was the help of all her work on the Scriptures, as well as the mind/ body research and study she had done and written about in her books, *The Right Connection* and *The Time is Right.*

Our friendship had been formed on a mutual search for truth. Her search started because she was infertile and wanted to have a baby. She decided she could change her belief system about the lack of pregnancy to one of having a baby simply by changing her mind through 1) her study of the mind/body connection in the eighties, and 2) her belief in His promise that He came to bring us life and life more abundantly.

(John 10:10) She gave birth to a darling baby boy, Dane, who is now a man of thirty-seven years. I have been blessed with his life, too, as his "adopted" aunt.

My search back then was for a way to live without guilt in the face of the deep, desperate sense of failure I felt about the divorce and the fact that I would not be able to provide my two adopted children with the perfect family.

So, out of a deep search for MORE, we found answers and have based our lives and friendship on them. We are deeply committed to what she calls "the empowerment principles." On these we "sit." And they are:

1) My mind creates my reality
2) I am always getting what I want
3) Everything happens for more for me
4) What I say to or about someone else is about me

At first these seem impossible, not only to understand but to apply. The first one, "My mind creates," means that I am NOT a victim of my reality. Everything I see with my natural eyes and have an opinion about is based on my perception. So, if I created cancer and "I am always getting what I want," I have to seriously ask, "Why?" The answer does not always come quickly, but *must* be something for my good. The worst, most horrible thing that can happen on earth, in God's eyes, can work out for something much greater than we can possibly see or know immediately.

What is the point here? I knew that the cancer, the treatment, the "marathon" was going to bring me *more*—more love, more strength, more purpose, and closer relationships with my daughters.

That "stone" I was sitting on was God's promise that He was in charge, and I was going to co-operate one hundred percent.

Pam's "holding up my arm" was a daily visit in the evenings and a reminder of who I was and am. She never wavered in her estimation that my faith would bring me through. It was a relief, many times, to know that is both how she saw me and how she knows me.

My other "arm holder" was Sue. I have written about how we met. Her ministering to me came through daily visits, starting in the morning to walk my dog, fix the flowers, and bring food. She also drove me to my appointments and had to wheel me into the offices in a wheelchair for the cancer treatments that took place months before the back surgery. She never once complained about her part in my journey and always reminded me of my faith. Her constant motto was "moving forward." It became our motto for every step of the way. We always saw the future being better and my being healed. Thus, the title of this book: *Moving Forward.*

It is important to read about what happened after the Israelis won the battle.

> And Joshua mowed down and disabled Amalek and his people with the sword.
>
> And the Lord said to Moses, Write this for a memorial in the book and rehearse it in the ears of Joshua, that I will utterly blot out the remembrance of Amalek from under the heavens.
>
> And Moses built an altar and called the name of it, The Lord is my Banner;
>
> And he said, Because [theirs] is a hand against the throne of the Lord, the Lord will have war with Amalek from generation to generation. (Exodus 17:13-16 TELB)

I take these words of the Lord to mean that whatever comes against us as His beloved, He will see to it that it will be blotted out. My cancer, her cancer, anyone's cancer, I believe can be blotted out by knowing and loving Him as the "Banner."

Some may disagree with me and recount stories of very good people dying of cancer, assuming that those incidents refute everything I have written. My answer is that what I am talking about is the power of the supernatural, not the natural. Each person's agreement with God about his/her future here and beyond is one only that individual and God can decide. For me, I sit happy and healed on the firm stone of His Word, surrounded by His angels, expecting to move forward in certainty that cancer has been blotted out forever in my body and my life.

In the Eye of the Storm

I couldn't figure it out right away. Pat is such a good friend and knows me so well. So, when she called to suggest I write a chapter on "The Eye of the Storm," I said, "OK," but nothing came immediately to mind. And then I knew. I was in the "eye" that very day, waiting for another doctor appointment to reassure me I was cancer-free despite the small amount of blood I had found days before. This happened almost a year to the day that I was officially declared "cancer free." I was exceedingly calm, but it definitely felt like being in the eye of a storm. I don't know how my friend knew that I needed to think about this.

What does "in the eye of a storm" feel like? It feels like the peace that passes understanding, confident of a good report yet with ominous thoughts intruding on my peace. I really didn't believe that anything was seriously wrong with me and that the doctor would give me a clean bill of health. But when you have gone through something like chemo and radiation, that experience never truly leaves. It isn't real in real time, but rather like a terrible storm you have gone through that could be coming again. I was shocked at how deep that sense of storm looming could be.

And then I thought more about the eye of the storm. This time I knew who to seek out for medical attention. I had made it through the storm before and could live through it again. I still had to wait for the doctor's opinion, just like waiting for the storm. And then Jesus in the storm came to mind. When His disciples called out in terror, He calmed the storm.

And a furious storm of wind [of hurricane proportions] arose, and the waves kept beating into the boat, so that is was already becoming filled. But He [Himself] was in the stern [of the boat], asleep on the [leather] cushion; and they awoke Him and said to Him, Master, do You not care that we are perishing? And He arose and rebuked the wind and said to the sea, Hush now! Be still (muzzled)! And the wind ceased (sank to rest as if exhausted by its beating) and there was [immediately] a great calm (a perfect peacefulness). (Mark 4:37-39 TELB)

Jesus was asleep! He didn't wake up from the horrific downpour, the huge waves rocking the boat back and forth, or the deafening sound of the storm. He only woke up when His beloved disciples called to Him to do something. I see so much promise in the passage. First of all, Jesus *knew* that the storm would not harm them. He knew that all was well, despite all the physical evidence to the contrary! Only when they called Him did He wake up to rebuke the wind and waves. He heard them over every other sound, just like He hears me.

I so relate to those disciples. I admit my fear. And yet there is Jesus with me in the boat. I know He is reassuring me that He is in charge and the outcome will be peace and not harm. He did not yell at the disciples for being afraid, just reminded them to use their faith. He calmed the physical storm and the storm of their fear. I find great comfort in that. Thank you, Lord, for showing me again that it is ok for me to have fear. You do not condemn me for that nor upbraid me. If I were You, I would probably tell me that by this time I should know better. Instead You soothe me, reminding me that we will get to the other side.

Visualizing the eye of the storm with storm clouds rolling about and circling inward, I can choose to see myself as a victim of what is coming or change my perspective by seeing myself at the center of power. I can see myself as a dot in a circle, drawing circles wider and wider within the circle until it is all filled with my circles with no more room for the storm clouds. Doing so uses the right and left hemispheres of my brain, allowing me to picture myself in control of my reaction to the storm. I can rebuke my fearful thoughts and encourage myself with the Word. "No weapon that is formed against you shall prosper...." (Is. 54:17 TELB)

Instead of shrinking in fear while the storm clouds get closer, I can expand my ability to see the whole picture—that Jesus has promised me healing and a long and lovely life.

> Who forgives [every one of] all your iniquities, Who heals [each one of you of] all your diseases, Who redeems your life from the pit and corruption, Who beautifies, dignifies, and crowns you with lovingkindness and tender mercy, Who satisfies your mouth, [your necessity and desire at your personal age and situation] with good so that your youth, renewed is like the eagle's [strong, overcoming, soaring]. (Psalm 103:3-5 TELB)

I am thinking that we all live in the eye of the storm each day. There will always be something to scare us, to test our commitment to His promises. Sometimes, I like to see myself huddled under the shadow of His wings, as it says in Psalm 91. Other times I prefer to see myself already at the other side. One of the best sermons I ever heard was one where the pastor insisted that we would never be in a terrifying storm unless we would make it to the other side. I had never thought it quite that way. Some may say that it is not always true that there is always an exit from the storm. There again, it is all about faith and perception. What some may see as no-exit, others may see as a Divine opportunity.

If we stop to think about it, we are always in the eye of a storm if we are with Him; then we are through the storm, and then to safety. Any place in the eye or in the storm, we are His and live in divine protection. Another thing to never forget is that He is in the boat with us!

One time I was really stressed and a friend asked me, "Margaret, don't you know that you are the like the apple of His eye?" I had never heard of that before, but the thought blessed me immeasurably. Deuteronomy 32:10 says that God found Jacob "...in a desert land, in the waste howling wilderness; he led him about, he instructed him, he kept him as the apple of his eye." (KJV)

If being in the eye of the storm while knowing that I am loved as the apple of His eye, I can trust and be calm. And that is what I intend to do.

ENOUGH!

My intention was to just walk over and say hello to my friend and neighbor, Pat. I knew she was in the process of deciding whether or not to undergo serious cancer surgery or just let it be, since it was just in the beginning stages. She had a lot on her mind and knew a lot about both medicine and all the risks she faced with either choice.

I had read an article about a woman who had reached out way beyond her church to make a difference in her city, state, and nation. She reminded me so much of Pat because Pat is a person who has done remarkable things in her life and ministry. She was an organizer of a huge refuge for the city's needy. She is smart, accomplished, and a great administrator – plus she has compassion and has overcome great grief from the loss of a beloved partner, her husband. I see so much potential in her—so much of what God could use her for and does even in our own little community. I wondered if she could see how important it is for her to stay alive, to be alive for all of us. I wondered if that article would inspire her to believe her healing had such an important purpose.

She was extremely gracious to me as always. She let me read her the article and present my case to her about the importance of her influence. Her response was interesting and made sense. "Margaret," she said, "I thought after my husband died, and I had processed it for over a year, that the sun was breaking through. I had a deep sense that more was coming but did not know what it was—just that it was something good. And then I discovered the blood, the diagnosis, and the acute awareness that I only have one kidney. That presents a lot of problems. The other thing is that I am in my late seventies, not in my fifties, like the lady in the article. I have less time and energy on my side."

I could so relate to the age consideration—not because I feel like aging or that I am able to do less, but because I have decided that I have accomplished things in the past that do not need doing over again. I have discovered less of the purpose of "DOING" and given more time and consideration to the purpose of "BEING." What I mean is that so much of what I did in the past was for the experience. I am now better equipped with wisdom because of all that. So being in my late seventies myself, I understood what she meant. Do I want or have I made the decision to live to be 120? YES. But do I have to redo what I have done in the past? No. God has been teaching me and leading me to see that I am more valuable as a role model of health, promise, love and wisdom than being busy creating something that would drain my time and energy. I am a teacher. He will and has been sending me students without my having to do anything but receive His guidance.

Back to Pat. She had a good point of being near the end of life with visions of a new endeavor which now seemed far beyond her reach. But she insisted that she knew God had something more for her. How did that factor into the reality of her serious diagnosis? How much time was left?

I really felt the dilemma and had been pondering it ever since another friend had informed me just that week that her health was very shaky. I was well aware of what Pat was saying about "time left." And somehow, somehow, out of her mouth came the words, the idea that whatever time there was left, it would be enough. We both sat in silence, until each of us repeated the word "enough." I felt the presence of God right there, filling us with the confidence that whatever happened or happens, He always gives us just enough. He will give us just the right amount of time to fulfill our purpose, to fulfill our destiny.

We were both so stunned with the Spirit. One of us mentioned that it was like the manna for the Israelites in the desert. They were promised and given manna just for the day. They were to take all they needed. If they took more than they needed, it would turn wormy. What a lesson for us! We were deeply assured that God would give us just the right amount of time in our lives to fulfill any desire of our hearts, which He had placed in there anyway.

I asked Pat if she wanted me to have a sign made for her home that said, "Enough." I had one made for Sue with the words "Moving Forward," and it turned out really nice. Pat just looked at me and said, "No, I have that word, 'enough,' written on my heart."

And I do too!

Second Corinthians 9:8 says:

> And God is able to make all grace (every favor and earthly blessing) come to you in abundance, so that you may always *and* under all circumstances *and* whatever the need be self-sufficient [possessing enough to require no aid or support and furnished in abundance for every good work and charitable donation]. (TELB)

THE TEA PARTY

Sometime during my healing process, I opened the armoire in my bedroom. Every time I opened that cupboard, I wondered to myself why I had all those tea cups and saucers. There were lots of them, all beautiful and yet collecting dust and lacking any real purpose. The days of hosting a tea party had long since passed. One time they were useful on many tables for a fabulous tea party luncheon at our Clubhouse. I couldn't see that ever happening again, not with the pain I was enduring and the treatment's side effects.

And then came Sophie. She is my granddaughter, nine years old now, who came with her mom, Catherine, to minister to me. At first, when I was very sick, she just came to the door of the bedroom and gently asked if there were anything I needed. Usually, there was not. I always thought that her mom had prompted her to ask. At that time, Sophie and I did not know each other well. But as time went by, and as I continued to improve, we became closer and closer.

During one visit, I had the armoire open to watch television from the bed. She came to the bed, so much closer to me than just peeking in like on the first visits. "Grandma, what are all those cups in there? They are beautiful!" I was curious that she even noticed and even more astounded at how much pleasure she took in examining each one. It seemed to me that it was time for a tea party. This one would be very small, a child and a sick grandmother sharing tea at the dining room table. She was thrilled when I suggested she set the table, choosing the cups she desired. I remember that I was very weak at the time, but nothing would keep me from that party.

The thing I noticed was that Sophie did not match the cups and saucers. Her eye and her design desire saw the cups and saucers unmatched. Sophie is very artistic like her mother, so I was a little surprised. And then I thought about it. Sometimes in life things just don't match up. What were the odds that a little nine-year old child, practically a stranger to me at the time, and a fragile, cancer-treated grandmother would be enjoying an incredible party? Only God could have arranged such a celebration.

Before the actual party, I got another idea. We were supposed to be "dressed up." How to do that? Well, I had shelves of costume jewelry in my closet, collecting dust just like the tea cups. Only then I saw a use for those, too! "Sophie," I suggested, "why don't you go into grandma's bedroom closet and pick out some jewelry for us?" She responded with glee and brought out large, dangling earrings, necklaces that didn't match the earrings, rings and even an evening bag which was one among many hanging on the wall. There I was in my nightgown with rhinestone earrings and gobs of pearls. She picked something daintier. We were quite the sight, and don't forget my head was shaved! My backside was tender with the healing stitches from the surgery, but my heart sang as I imagined us in an elegant tearoom enjoying what we both loved best: each other.

There were more surprises in store for me. Sipping the grape juice "tea," Sophie instructed me how to hold the cup with the thumb and the middle finger. I was to hold the saucer with the other hand and place it underneath the cup. I was astounded! "How do you know that?" I asked. She replied that she had read about it in a book in her school library. Both the teacher and the proud grandmother in me beamed.

That's when I decided we should introduce ourselves with made-up names. I was Madame Kuzinski, and she was Rose. The next thing we had to do was tell about our made-up places of origin. Very interesting. I was from Russia and an actress. She was more realistic and said, "California" and that she was a horsewoman, which was really the truth. It opened up an opportunity to ask her about horses. I was entertained with a fifteen-minute overview of horses, their features, and all their various types. I was fascinated by her knowledge.

That tea party introduced a whole new dimension to our relationship. I had a granddaughter who loved beautiful things like me and loved to share. Sometime during the party, she asked if she could open the drawer in the china cabinet. It revealed a sterling silver lazy Susan and lots of other treasures. She handled each one with care and reverence. They were gifts I had received forty-five years before, hidden in a cupboard and unused. There she was, lovingly appreciating their beauty. I was touched to the core. I had thought that no one would like those things ever again. She was breathing new life into my past by respecting their value in the present.

That is the message I believe God wants us to receive. He keeps granting us opportunities to love and with them new connections and new life. The only time I seriously considered the thought of dying throughout this whole ordeal was before the back operation. However, I thought about my legacy all the time. Having tea with Sophie showed me that my idea of my legacy was way too small. She showed me more possibility for the future than I could ever have imagined. And it all took place during a tea party!

I learned something else that day as well. For some time, I had been criticizing myself for having bought so many things in the past, too much stuff. And that day, I realized that those things had given me great joy at the time. They symbolized my quest for beauty. I also believe that they were an outlet for happiness while I was still in a state of lack and loss before the restoration of my relationships with my children. I had been praying Isaiah 54 for years, about peace coming to my children and my children's children. That afternoon, my prayer was answered. And once again, God was reminding me that "There is now no condemnation to them which are in Christ Jesus...." (Rom. 8:1 KJV)

It took the eyes of a child to remind me, again, of His forgiveness, His abiding love, and His promise.

Responding to the Need

Presently, there are two benches outside the front doors of our church. They are there because I needed to sit down while waiting for Pam to pick me up after the service. It was that difficult to walk to the car. "If only I could sit someplace," I thought. The pain was too great to stand.

I had asked my pastor about getting benches for the outside. His response was immediate: "Of course." He had simply not been aware of the need. Just like me. I had walked through those doors for years, never once thinking about needing a place to sit down. That was before the pain and the treatment. We often don't see needs in others until we experience them ourselves.

Pastor Jason does see the needs in others, and, in fact, has dedicated his ministry to doing something about it. His passion is to win souls. His method is to embrace anyone and everyone who has a need. The first need, I believe he would say, is the need for Jesus. To reach out to those, he embraces everyone, especially through his message of healing.

My urgent need had been for healing, and my pastor responded. I experienced the prayer and the anointing oil he and his wife, Kelli, ministered to me. I felt it and heard his words over me. He spoke that I would be transformed, maybe not always feeling comfortable in my own skin, but at the same time receiving healing as a free gift from the Lord. His words were prophetic. Many times, as I have written about, I did not even recognize myself. My image of myself was being changed as God did His perfect work in me.

During that time of healing, I always counted on knowing, really knowing, that Pastor Jason *believed* in healing. There was no doubt in his mind that my liberation from the disease and pain would occur. I could visualize his faith. It was that obvious, that palpable. Yes, he offers many testimonies of how people in our church and community have been healed. Those accounts helped to build confidence that it could happen to me. It is the way he delivered those testimonies, from his heart, that reinforced my faith. He is steadfast in his belief. He is rock solid that healing is not only possible but real, in real time, in real life. He has experienced many of those healings himself and shares those miracles. I was curious about the meaning of the name "Jason," and googled it. The name, I found out, means "healer."

Yes, Jason is a healer because he believes in miracles, not just in the time of Jesus but right now. His belief—his looking me in the eye with the confidence of God's promises—helped me to keep my faith. I am forever grateful. He saw the need in me, the need to sustain my faith during the ordeal, and he has never wavered in his vision of the outcome, my complete restoration.

One of the benches outside the church has a plaque which reads, "Be still and know that I am God." (Ps. 46:10) The other bench has a plaque which reads, "Come to me all who are weary, and I will give you rest." (Matt. 11:28) Jason encouraged me to rest in His love. I did. I am healed and very grateful.

THE CIRCLE OF POWER

It made sense to me that she worked with flowers. She herself is like a beautiful flower, open to the light of God's Word. I met her in a prayer group years before and knew she had special perception and insight, always delivered in a quiet yet confident way. She saw into the Word in a way none of the rest of us did just like she could see how to arrange a group of flowers, creating something even more beautiful.

So, when Maureen approached me with prayers for healing, I accepted immediately and with gratitude. She had them written out in her own handwriting, making them all the more personal. Then she suggested an anointing with oil after a church service with the pastor and his wife. I immediately agreed. We did it in the back of the church. She and my friends surrounded me. I felt the power of their intention for my healing. It came over me like a quiet force.

I had almost forgotten about that time. But yesterday, I was reading Acts 14:19-20. Paul had been preaching, and some of the people were offended so decided to stone him. He was at the point of death.

> ...having stoned Paul, [they] drew him out of the city, supposing he had been dead. Howbeit, as the disciples stood round about him, he rose up and came into the city, and the next day he departed with Barnabas to Derbe. (KJV)

Paul was dying. That is how it appeared. Yet, by the power of the circle of his believing friends with love and prayer, he was revived and restored. Right next to that verse in my Bible I had written the following: "Just like my prayer of 1-20-2019 for healing with Maureen, Jason, Kelli, Pam, Monique, Tori, and others."

I am so happy I was reminded of that occasion. Not only is that circle of friends dear to me, but the power in it is supernatural. Georgiann told me the other day that besides calling me about the book club, she was constantly praying for me. She is not the only one. I see all those prayers then and now as joined in another kind of circle, a circle of light around those of us who so need strength. Prayer is real. It works. The Bible says it this way in James.

> Is any among you afflicted? let him pray. Is any merry? let him sing psalms.

> Is any sick among you? let him call for the elders of the church; and let them pray over him, anointing him with the oil in the name of the Lord:

> And the prayer of faith shall save the sick, and the Lord shall raise him up; and if he have committed sins, they shall be forgiven him.

> Confess your faults one to another, and pray one for another that ye may be healed. The effectual fervent prayer of a righteous man availeth much. (James 5:13-16 KJV)

Often those prayers can come from complete strangers. One of those was the lady on the end of the prayer line at Dennis Burke's Ministry. He had preached at our church, and I followed him with a daily devotional online. Right before the surgery, lying on the couch in a lot of pain and filled with anxiety, I called that ministry for prayer. A lady, Annie, answered and gave me such a personal prayer and made such a personal connection with me, that I was renewed.

I received the partner letter from that ministry today. It says that we must have courage and that one of the definitions of courage is to "have a buoyant spirit." The word, "buoyant," resonated deep within me. If you take a ball and try to submerge it, you cannot. It demands to come to the top. That is how I see the Holy Spirit in me. At my request, He comes to the top, overcoming any fear or anxiety with peace. That is what that phone conversation with Annie accomplished: peace. Much later, after the successful operation, I called to give her my testimony. She relayed it to Dr. Burke who referenced it in a letter to his partners.

I can visualize a pebble thrown into a lake. When it hits the water, circles form, moving out and even further out. That is what the circle of prayer does as it moves into places farther and deeper than even intended. God has given us prayer and each other to share its blessings. I am grateful for all of it.

PERKS

Carolyn, my mentor and encourager, looked at me in disbelief. I had told her that I was going to write about the "perks" of having cancer. "What 'perks' could there possibly be with cancer?" she asked.

Then I explained that the word "cancer" is universal. Everyone either has or had cancer, or knows someone who has. Thus, once the word is said, an immediate relationship of disaster, sadness, fear, hopelessness, pain, and maybe hope is stirred, and a conversation can get started, even with complete strangers.

And that is what I am after: the conversation. Because in my case, I have survived and am thriving. Once we get to talking about cancer, then the conversation can easily be led to my experience with cancer and all the horror that went with it. This only presents the opportunity to talk about my walk of faith and how only God could have brought me through. Yes, cancer has allowed me a means or a deeper method of spreading the gospel! I use my testimony to give Him the praise and the glory.

Just today, I was at Panda Express where Maria was serving up the order. She had not seen me in a long time because for a while I could not even stand in a line to order food. I told her about the cancer and back surgery and that I am a "walking miracle."

She said, "I noticed that your long hair is gone. You look different. I didn't recognize you at first."

"Yes," I replied. "It was the chemo that took my hair, but I love this new look. And I give God all the credit for the miracles that have taken place in my life since I saw you last."

I took my food, added the tea, and was on my way out of the restaurant when a lovely couple called me over to their table. "We heard you talking about your miracles," he said.

"Yes, I have had many. Do either of you have cancer or know someone who does?"

"No, no. We don't. Just that a friend of ours does."

"Well," I said, "I just want you to tell her that you met a lady who has and had radical hope, and she has recovered. Just tell your friend to surrender to the strength of God. To relax and keep believing that He will heal her." There was a look in the lady's eyes as she watched me tell her this. She, I am sure, felt the healing spirit flow from me, and I was reassured that I am on the right path, lifting others up with hope. Before we parted, the gentleman asked if I thought that what I ate had anything to do with my "miracle." Actually, I know a lot of people who treat cancer with certain diets. I never did. The truth is that I did not feel like eating very much. It was work. However, I did take Communion each day and believe that Jesus left us Communion for the healing of our bodies.

Joseph Prince first introduced the idea to me that the bread and the wine of Communion were given for two distinct purposes. The wine was His blood, which reminds us that He made us righteous. We do not ever have to prove that we are righteous. He did it all for us. The bread has its own purpose, that of healing our bodies. I had never made that distinction until about five years ago when I started taking Communion at home each day. It made sense to me that because Jesus spent so much of His time on earth healing, it had to be a priority for Him. Why would He leave and not give us something for healing? It just made sense that He would. Therefore, it is not a stretch for me to believe in the power of daily Communion. I look at the bread, and I paraphrase Isaiah 53:5, saying, "by His stripes I am healed." He took that scourging for my healing. If He did it, and I am as He is in this world, then I have to be healed. Believing in this strengthened my faith to a great degree; therefore, the question about "food" and "diet" was a good one. I did practice the diet of healing with Communion, taking it as the bread of life.

Another opportunity for witnessing came when I was on the table having a bone density test. During the medical procedure I answered all the questions about my medical history. Then out of the blue, the technician asked, "Do you think you could have coffee or lunch with me? I would like to talk more about your healing and how you think. How were you able to go through so much and come out looking and feeling so well?" I couldn't even see the girl. She was behind me. It was as if a voice out of nowhere were asking me for more. What did I say to have her be prompted to ask a perfect stranger, a patient, for more information about her (and my), belief in God? I really was surprised but, of course, was eager to agree to a time and place that we could meet. What would be the purpose? To use what God had helped me through to deepen my faith so that I could share with her. To show her what is possible in this lifetime for hope and joy.

We did meet. She had a lot of questions, and we found that our lives were very similar. We were both rejected women. Our husbands had left us for "another woman." The theme of rejection and loss was deep in her, and I could relate all too well. I have written that the basis for my rectal cancer, I believe, was the humiliation and failure of the divorce, at the bottom of my psyche, creating disease in my body. I see now that the cancer healing process was to restore my relationship with Him and to remind me how He loves me. To show me that the divorce did not leave me in lack. It provided me with opportunities to have more of His love, and the greatest "perk" of all is to be able to share that experience and that love.

God restores everything. I believe that He restores what He never took away. The reason I say this is because the only one who can take away anything is myself by the way I perceive it. By committing to the principle that everything happens for a reason for more, I can believe that God will always fulfill my needs; I need never be in lack, for He is my Provider and my Sustainer.

There are other "perks" I have enjoyed because of cancer; I have established many relationships which seemed impossible before. I have an abiding sense of hope that my life has a purpose and a destiny. I have gained insight into restoration. I believe that I should look ten years older than I do after enduring the severe pain in my leg before and during surgery, chemo, and radiation. I would have thought that the stress from all that ordeal would have aged me so much. And yet, everyone who sees me cannot believe how well and young I look. I can't either. It isn't only the cute, short haircut; it is a radiance from deep within that the Holy Spirit is alive and well and living inside of my body, eagerly waiting to do everything possible to keep me healthy and happy. I am a living Temple and have tremendous respect for His abiding in me. It is my job to recognize His presence, to listen and to follow His lead. And that is my commitment and my joy. "For by me [Wisdom from God] your days shall be multiplied, and the years of your life shall be increased." (Proverbs 9:11 TELB)

Another "perk" is that I have the joy of sharing His wonderful healing power for the rest of my life. My desire is to fulfill His command in Mark 16:15: "And He said to them, Go into all the world and preach *and* publish openly the good news (the gospel) to every creature [of the whole human race]." (TELB)

To Be Continued...

Just as I was about to finish this last chapter, and on the very day of the one-year anniversary of my back surgery, the pain in my other leg hit hard and caused excruciating pain. Once again, I was in the eye of the storm. I wanted to scream. I wanted to worry about whether or not the operation had really worked.

I saw this attack as an ambush by the devil to try to erode my faith and stop this writing. I also saw it as another opportunity to keep asking God for His Divine protection. I went through the MRI, and it proved nothing wrong. I thanked God for His healing power. I also thanked Him for reminding me that healing is never over. It is a continuous thing like life itself. And that is why I believe He told us the following in Matthew 7:7-8.

> Keep on asking and it will be given you; keep on seeking and you will find; keep on knocking [reverently] and [the door] will be opened to you.
>
> For everyone who keeps on asking receives; and he who keeps on seeking finds; and to him who keeps on knocking [the door] will be opened. (TELB)

I believe we are to keep on believing in our healing and well-being and never take it for granted. A certain healing is done at a certain time. However, time is continuous, and therefore our believing must be also—keeping our faith, seeking His face, receiving His promises – *always* and *continually*, and that is why "To Be Continued" has become a way of life. The "To Be Continued" is the constant faith in knowing I AM HEALED and accepting the joy of it!

A week later, I found some blood. Another attack. The doctor found that it was the result of radiation damage. I do not have cancer again. I keep on asking, giving thanks, trusting and praising Him for His fulfilled promises.

> Trust (lean on, rely on, and be confident) in the Lord and do good; so you shall dwell in the land and feed surely on His faithfulness, and truly you shall be fed.
>
> Delight yourself also in the Lord, and He will give you the desires and secret petitions of your heart.
>
> Commit your way to the Lord [roll and repose each care of your load on Him]; trust (lean on, and be confident) also in Him and He will bring it to pass. (Psalm 37:3-5 TELB)

And then I can and do say—constantly, "Many, O Lord my God are the wonderful works which you have done, and your thoughts toward us; no one can compare with you! If I should declare and speak of them, they are too many to be numbered." (Ps. 40:5 TELB)

The key word in that last paragraph is "say." I know and keep reminding myself how important it is to keep **saying** His Words. Right before this went to print, my pastor, Kelli Anderson, Pastor Jason's wife, wrote her book called *I SPEAK JESUS*. The timing was perfect because her work demonstrates not only how important it is to fight the devil with the Words of Jesus, but to do it all the time, continuously. Using examples from her own life, she tells of the miracles that happened when she spoke His Words into her situations. We cannot be reminded enough of the power of the Word of God. It must be in our hearts and come from our mouths **all the time**. Pastor Kelli and Pastor Jason did that for me from the diagnosis to my complete healing – so I know it works!

Just like Psalm 40:5 says: the "wonderful works" of the Lord if I speak them are "too many to be numbered."

He gets all the Glory!

THE LAST WORD

It is my deepest wish that something in this book has lifted your spirit and given you hope. Carolyn told me that I have "radical hope." Maybe having "radical hope" is what helped me the most, and I encourage you to have it, too. The Bible puts it this way in Hebrews 10:35: "Cast not away therefore your confidence, which hath great recompence of reward." (KJV)

It is my prayer that you always:

> **Remember.**
> **Remember.**
> **Remember.**
> **He wants us healed.**
> **He loves us.**
> **He has promised us healing.**
> **He always keeps His Word.**

Psalm 107 repeats His reassurance 4 times.

> Then they cried to the Lord in their trouble, and He delivered them out of their distresses. (Verse 6)

> Then they cried to the Lord in their trouble, and He saved them out of their distresses. (Verse 13)

Then they cry to the Lord in their trouble, and He delivers them out of their distresses. (Verse 19)

Then they cry to the Lord in their trouble, and He brings them out of their distresses. (Verse 28)

It also says, in the Psalm, verse 14, that "He brought them out of darkness and the shadow of death and broke apart the bonds that held them." (TELB)

He deserves all the praise.

WHO IS MARGARET LANG?

Margaret Lang is a mom, a friend, a former English teacher of thirty years, a real estate agent, and now an author. For many years she has taught and mentored students and friends always sharing her belief in possibility. She has just experienced cancer and transformed her life by successfully meeting that challenge. Hopefully, chronicling her journey will bring faith and hope to many others.

Asked what her purpose is in life, she refers to Psalm 26:7: *"That I may make the voice of my thanksgiving heard and may tell of all Your wondrous works." (TELB)*

ACKNOWLEDGEMENTS

I am filled with gratitude for everyone involved in this project. The writing of it was almost as much of a healing grace as everything else involved.

I especially want to thank Carolyn Jones Schock for inspiring me to do it, encouraging me, directing me and loving me. I am forever grateful.

I am DEEPLY grateful to Georgiann Crouse, Pat Palmer and Sherilyn Matzke for assisting in editing the book. That job, I believe, is one of the hardest, and they did a wonderful job.

Thank you to my daughter, Catherine, for the Brushstroke Cross in Heart design used at the beginning of each chapter.

I am abundantly blessed to have two dear friends who are also authors, and their work is truly God inspired. Using their books has helped me tremendously, and I am so grateful.

Pastor Kelli wrote *I SPEAK JESUS* which can be ordered on Amazon.

Pam Emmer wrote *THE RIGHT CONNECTION: Moving Through Life Without Limitation* and *THE TIME IS RIGHT: Today's Tools For Tomorrow's Leaders*. Both books can be obtained by emailing Pam at **pemmer@cox.net.**

And thank you to the staff at Xulon Press for all their help and support.

CPSIA information can be obtained
at www.ICGtesting.com
Printed in the USA
FSHW021527020920
73506FS

9 781632 210265